Penny Stocks

2nd Edition

The Definitive Guide to Penny Stocks Profits

Top Strategies and Secrets of Penny Stocks Trading

Winston J. Duncan

Table of Contents

Introduction

A cautious investor who is interested in making a profit in the quickest time possible may choose to invest in penny stocks. Although these stocks are known to be high in risk, they have the advantage of being low in value, which means that you can manage and possibly afford a loss with penny stocks. This results in an increase in bravado or boldness, even for the cautious investor, as there is a real possibility of making a great profit.

However, this is not possible if you do not have a strategy in mind. To begin with, penny stocks are challenging and far from a get rich quick scheme. They can give you a great return in excess of 100% if you are patient and take the time to create and follow a trading strategy.

They are designed to be shorter tern in nature that the traditional stocks, which is something that any penny stock trader should keep in mind. Using the strategy to buy and hold these stocks could lead to significant losses as the stocks can change their values within seconds.

This book contains that best strategies that you can follow, especially if your focus is on making a lasting profit. You will also find some secrets that will give you the edge when trading, whether you are experienced or are just starting out in trading.

Penny stocks should have a place within your portfolio, as they are thrilling to trade in, and they also offer significant returns when the right trading decision is made.

CHAPTER 1

First things first –
Basics of Stocks and Options

In order to understand options, you must first understand stocks as they are interlinked but different. Being a business owner without having to show up at work using stocks and options takes some understanding of both, and without that understanding, you could end up losing a lot of money and wasting a lot of time.

The dream of being a business owner who doesn't have to leave home and still make a lot of money is not a pipe dream. Stocks are the cornerstone of any investment portfolio. Having a solid understanding of this piece of the puzzle is a must.

If you take a look at the time over the last few decades, you can see that the interest in the stock market has grown greatly. The stock market used to be a toy for the rich to play a game, but now it's a way to grow your wealth and make a lot of money. This demand joined with advances in the trading technology has created a way for markets to allow almost anyone to own stocks and options.

Unfortunately, while they are popular, most people don't really understand stocks. A lot is learned from their friends, peers, and family rather than actually talking to a stock broker or even picking up a book about stocks and options. But you don't have to be that person. You chose to pick up this book and educate yourself about this topic.

Most of what you will hear from family and friends pertains to people *losing* money in the stock market rather than *making* it. Be aware that this sensationalism comes from the misinformation of get rich quick schemes and scams. Stocks are not the magic answer to wealth, but they can make you wealthy if you know what you're doing. Stocks will create massive amounts of wealth, maybe for you, but they do not come without risk. Understanding the stock market and where you're putting your money is going to make you a lot better at making money.

Now, an investor's portfolio usually includes items such as stocks, bonds, and mutual funds, but there is a fourth option at their disposal! These are known as options. Options are versatile, and that's where their power lies. They allow the trader to adapt or adjust their position according to a number of situations that might come about. Options are able to be speculative or conservative. You can do just about anything from protecting a position or declining or outright betting on the movement of the index or market.

However, the versatility of options is not without cost. They are complex and can be riskier than a stock. That's why you'll see plenty of disclaimers telling you that options trading is very risky and should only be done with risk capital.

If someone tells you that options' trading does not come with risks, then they are not to be trusted. Even if you know what you're doing, you can still lose a substantial amount of money, so be careful. Due to this risk, many will suggest that you forget they exist and steer away from them, but being ignorant of another type of investment option will put you in a weak position.

Even if you do not decide to invest in options, you ought to understand them so that you know what is happening if someone makes an offer to you. Not learning how they function is just as dangerous as investing in them without being educated about them, so I urge you to read forward even if you are not willing to take the risks.

Most multi-national, multi-million dollar companies offer options to employees and others so you may want to pay attention.

Before we discuss options, I am going to go into stocks in case you're completely new to the stock market world. Even if you're not, you may want to continue reading in case you learn something new.

What are Stocks?

In short, a stock is a share in the ownership of a company, but they are really much more than this. They represent a claim to the company's earnings, as well as assets. When you acquire more stock, you acquire a greater part of the company's ownership. Stocks are also known as equity and shares, so be aware that when someone uses those terms they are really talking about stocks.

When you hold a company's stocks, you are a shareholder or a partial owner of the company, and that means you have a claim to everything the company owns. Usually, this is a small claim. So technically, you own a sliver of every piece of furniture, trademark, and contact the company has. As an owner, you will get some of the company's earnings and will be able to have voting rights if they are attached to the stock.

Stocks are represented by certificates, which are fancy pieces of paper that prove you are a partial owner. You usually won't see these documents during our modern times because they are recorded electronically, and this is known as holding shares in street name. This is done so that they are easier to trade. In the past, when you wanted to sell a share, you had to physically take the certificate down to the brokerage office. Now, all you have to do is click a link on a website or make a phone call. Life is much easier for everyone involved.

When you're a shareholder in a public company, it doesn't mean that you have a say in the daily operations of the business. Instead, you can vote once per share in order to elect a board of directors at annual meetings, and that's the extent of your say in the company. For instance, if you're a shareholder in Microsoft, you don't get to call up Bill Gates and tell him that you think the company should create a program or change a program. In the same line of thinking, if you're the shareholder of a beer company, you don't get to just walk in grab a free case of beer.

The management of the company is going to increase the value of the company for the shareholders. If that doesn't happen, the shareholders can vote to remove the management in theory. In reality, an individual investor like you or me would not own enough shares in order to have a material influence on the company. It's the really large investors that have the say-so in a company.

For an ordinary shareholder, not being able to have a say-so in the managing of the company is not that big of a deal. After all, the idea is to not have to work to make the money. The importance of being someone who holds shares is that you're entitled to part of the company's profits and you have a claim on the assets. Profits can be paid on the forms of dividends. The more shares you have, the larger your portion of the profits is. Your claim on the assets is only relevant if the company goes under. In the case of liquidation, you will get what is left over after the creditors are paid.

Another important part of the stock is its limited liability. That means that as an owner of a stock, you're not liable if the company cannot pay its debt. Other companies that are set up as partnerships are set up so that if the company goes bankrupt, the other partner or shareholder can be liable to the creditors. They can come after you personally and sell off your car, house, furniture, and other worldly possessions in order to get the debt that is owed to the company. Owning a stock means that the maximum you can lose is the value of the investment. Even if a company goes bankrupt, you will never lose personal assets.

Debt versus Equity

So why does a company issue stock? Why would the founders want to share the profits with thousands when they could keep it all to themselves?

The reason is that, at some point, most companies need to raise money. In order to do this, they can borrow from someone or they can sell part of their company, which is issuing stocks. A company can borrow by obtaining a loan from a bank, or they can issue bonds. Both methods are under the umbrella of debt financing.

On one hand, issuing a stock is known as equity financing. Distributing stock is good for the company because it doesn't require that the company pay back any money they borrowed or make payments on interest as they go. All they have to do is pay out dividends when the stock declares they will. The first sale of stocks is known as the initial public offering or IPO.

You may not think that it's important you understand the difference between a company that finances through debt and finances through equity, but you would be in the wrong if you did. When you purchase a debt investment like a bond, you are assured the return of the principal amount you paid as well as assured interest payments. This isn't the situation with equity investment.

When you become an owner, you undertake the risk of the company not making it, just like a small business owner is not guaranteed to be successful. As an owner, your claim to the assets is less than the claim of the creditors. This means that if the company goes under and liquidates their assets, you will not be able to touch any of it until the creditors have been paid first. This is known as absolute priority. Shareholders can earn a lot if the company is successful, but they can also lose a lot if the company is not.

Risk

I believe I would be amiss if I did not emphasize that there is not a guarantee when you purchase an individual stock. Some companies are going to pay out dividends, but others are not. And there is not an obligation to pay out dividends even if a company has traditionally done so. Without dividends, an investor can only make money through the appreciation of the stock on the open market. On the downside, a stock that goes bankrupt leaves the stockholder with nothing.

While the risk might sound very negative and turn you away from the stock market altogether, there is a bright side. Taking on a greater risk will demand a greater return on investment. That is why stocks have outperformed other investment options like bonds and savings accounts. Over the long-term, an investment stock has an average return of around ten to twelve percent.

Now that you're aware of the risk involved with stocks let's talk about the different types.

CHAPTER 2

Types of Stocks

There are two different types of stocks, common and preferred. Depending on how much you're investing, you will have the choice between the two.

Common

Common is the one that is usually referred to during pleasant conversation. Common stock is most of what a company puts out when they issue stock. They represent a share in the company and a claim to dividends or a portion of the profits. Investors of this type of stock get one vote per share when electing a board member, who will oversee the major decisions that are made by management and the company.

Over the long term, common stock yields a higher return than almost any other investment when it comes to capital growth. This higher return can come at a higher cost because common stocks have the most risk. If a company goes bankrupt, you will not receive anything until the creditors are paid. In addition, you won't receive anything until the preferred shareholders are compensated.

Preferred

A preferred stock is going to come with the same degree of ownership in the company, but it's not going to come with the same voting rights.

With a preferred share, an investor is going to guarantee a fixed dividend forever. This is unlike a common stock because a common stock has a variable dividend that is never guaranteed. Another advantage is that if liquidation occurs, a preferred shareholder is going to be paid before a common one. However, a preferred shareholder will still only be paid after the creditors are paid. Preferred stock can also be callable, which means the company has the option to purchase back the stock from the shareholder at a premium.

Some consider a preferred stock to be more representative of a debt than equity. A good way to think of a share like this is to think of it like a share that is between a bond and a common share.

Classes of Stock

While the common and preferred stocks are the two main forms, it's also possible for a company to customize their different classes of stock however they want. The most common reason to do this is because the company wants the voting power to remain with a certain group. If this is the case, the company will give different voting rights to different shares. For example, one class could be held by a select group who are given ten votes a share rather than just one.

When there's more than one class, the classes are designated Class A and Class B. The different forms can be represented by an a or b being placed behind the ticker symbol of the stock, such as BRKa or BRKb.

Companies can create many different classes of stocks, so be aware of what you're looking at and always do the research on the company's website.

CHAPTER 3

Trading Stocks

When you go to purchase a stock or trade a stock, you're most likely going to go to an exchange, which a place where a buyer and seller meet in order to decide on a price. Some are physical locations and transactions are carried out on the actual trading floor. You've most likely seen some photographs of trading floors, where the traders are throwing their arms in the air, waving, yelling, and signaling. It really is a wild ride. There is another type of exchange, though. This is a virtual exchange that is made up of a network of computers where traders discuss and trade electronically.

The purpose of a stock market is to enable the exchange of stocks or securities between the buyers and sellers, which reduces the risk of investing. Just imagine how difficult it would be if you had to call around yourself in order to sell your stock. Really, the stock market is nothing more than a sophisticated market place where buyers and sellers are linked together.

Before I move on, I should tell you the difference between the primary and secondary market. The primary market is where the company will sell their IPO's or securities, and in the secondary market, investors will trade or sell a previously-issued security without the issuing company being involved. The secondary market is usually what most are referring to when they say 'stock market.' It's imperative to understand that the trading of a company's stock is not going to involve the company at all.

There are two famous stock markets in the United States, the New York Stock Exchange, and NASDAQ.

The New York Stock Exchange

This is the most prestigious of stock markets across the globe and goes by NYSE. It was founded over two hundred years ago in 1792 when the Buttonwood Agreement was signed by twenty-four New York City stockbrokers and merchants. Currently, this stock market is the market of choice in America due to its big name company players.

It's the first type of exchange where most of the trading is done face to face on the floor. This is also denoted to as a listed exchange. Orders will come in through a brokerage firm where members of the exchange are located and it will flow down to the floor brokers who will go to the specific spot where the stock trading is taking place. At this location, which is also known as the trading post, there is a person who is known as a specialist whose job is to match up the buyers and sellers.

The prices are set using the auction method. The current price is the highest amount the buyer is willing to pay and the lowest price where someone is willing to sell. Once the trade is completed, the details are sent to the brokerage firm, who will notify the investor who put in the order. While there is human contact in the process, computers still play a huge role in the process.

The NASDAQ

This is the second type of exchange and it's a virtual type called over the counter or OTC market. The NASDAQ is the most popular of this type. An OTC market does not have a central location or a floor broker. The trading takes place through computers and telecommunications with a network of dealers. In history, the largest companies listed with the NYSE while the other second place companies would trade on other exchanges. However, the tech boom of the late 1990's changed all of this. Now the NASDAQ is home to many big companies like Cisco, Microsoft, Dell, Intel, and Oracle. Therefore, NASDAQ is a serious competitor of NYSE.

The NASDAQ brokerages seem to behave as market makers for different stocks. A market maker is something that provides a continuous bid and ask price in a set percentage spread for shares. They can match up buyers and sellers directly, but they usually maintain an inventory of shares in order to meet the demands of investors.

Other Exchanges

The next largest exchange is the American Stock Exchange in the United States, also known as AMEX. AMEX used to be an alternative to NYSE, but that role is now filled by NASDAQ. NASD, the National Association of Securities Dealers, is the parent of NASDAQ. NASD bought AMEX in 1998. Therefore, now almost all of the trading is small-cap stocks and derivatives.

There are numerous stock exchanges that are located in almost every country across the globe. American markets are the largest, but they are still just a fraction of the investment opportunities across the globe. The other two financial hubs are London and Hong Kong, home of the London Stock Exchange and the Hong Kong Stock Exchange respectively.

The final place that's worth a mention is the OTCBB or Over the Counter Bulletin Board. This term refers to companies that are too small to meet the listing requirements of a regulated market, including the NASDAQ. The OTCBB is the home of the penny stocks because there is almost no regulation. This makes investing in the OTCBB market riskier than most.

Now that you're aware of how stocks are traded let's look at the different causes of drops and rises in prices.

CHAPTER 4

Causes of Stock Prices Dropping and Rising

The stock prices are always fluctuating on a daily basis due to different market forces. Market forces are the supply and demand of the stocks. If more potential shareholders want to purchase a stock than sell it, then the price will go up. At the same time, if more people would want to sell the stock rather than buy it, there is a greater supply than demand, and the price falls.

Understanding supply and demand is pretty simple. What is difficult to understand is what makes people want one stock over another. This can come down to figuring out what news is positive for companies and what is negative. There are numerous answers to this complication, and just about any investor is going to have their own strategies and ideas.

With that being said, the main theory is that the price fluctuation of a stock indicates what the investors feel the company is worth. Do not think that a company's value is only in the stock price. The value of the company is the market capitalization, which is the stock price times the number of shares that are outstanding. For example, let's say a company trades at $200 per share and has 3 million shares outstanding, and has a lesser value than a company that trades at $100 that has 6 million shares outstanding. Two hundred dollars multiplied by three million shares is six hundred million dollars. One hundred dollars multiplied by six million shares is six hundred million dollars. Therefore, they are pretty equal.

To further make things more difficult, the price of the stock is not only reflective of the company's current value, but also the growth that investors want to see in the future. The most important factor that is part of the company's value is its earnings. Earnings are the profit the company makes, and a company cannot survive the long run without them. It makes sense if you think about it. If a company doesn't make money, it isn't going to stay in business. Public companies are required to report their earnings quarterly. Wall Street pays rapt attention to these during the earnings seasons. The reason is that an analyst will base the future value of the company on the earnings projection. If a company's results are greater, the price jumps up. If the results are disappointing, then the price falls.

However, it's not just earnings that will change the sentiment toward a stock. It would be pretty easy if that were the case! During the dot-com era, dozens of internet companies capitalized in billions of dollars without actually making a profit. As most of you know, the valuations of the companies did not hold and the internet businesses saw their values contract to just a fraction of their peak. Still, the fact that the prices moved demonstrates that there are factors other than the current earnings that influence the stock market.

Investors developed hundreds of ratios, variables, and indicators. Many of you may have already heard of the price/earnings ratio, or the Chaikin oscillator.

So why do the prices change for stocks? The best answer is that no one really knows. Some believe it's not possible to predict how a stock will change while some believe that making a chart and looking at the past price movements will tell them. The only thing that is certain is that stocks are always changing.

The important things you should have gathered are:

- That at the most basic level, supply and demand in the stock market is going to determine the stock price.

- Price multiplied by the number of shares outstanding is the value of the company. Comparing just the share price of two companies is not going give you good, valid information.

- Earnings should be what affect an investor's value report of a company, but there are other indicators that they use in order to predict a stock price. Remember, it's the investors who ultimately affect the price of stocks.

- There are numerous theories that attempt to explain the way the stock prices move and why they do, but there is not any one theory that has a good explanation.

Now that you know how the stock market prices fluctuate let's look at how to purchase stocks.

CHAPTER 5

Buying Stocks

You now know what a stock is and some about the principles behind the market they're traded in, but how do you actually purchase a stock? Fortunately, a trip to the stock market in New York City is not in your near future unless you really want it to be. There are two main ways to purchase stocks.

Brokerage

Using a brokerage is the most common way to purchase stocks. They come in two different styles. Full-service brokerages will offer you expert advice and will manage your accounts, but they do charge a hefty price. Discount brokerages will offer very little personal attention to your portfolio, but they are cheaper.

It used to be that only the wealthy were able to afford brokers because they were expensive and full-service only. When the internet came about, the explosion of online discount brokers also made an appearance. Thanks to the internet, almost anyone can afford to invest in the market.

DIPs and DRIPs

DRIPs are dividend reinvestment plans and DIPs are direct investment plans. These plans are how individual companies, at a low cost, allow a shareholder to purchase stock directly from them. DRIPs are an excellent way to invest a small amount into a company at a regular interval.

Purchasing stocks is not difficult at all. All you have to do is go online and sign up on a reputable website in order to start trading.

CHAPTER 6

To business - Penny Stocks Basics

These are an amazing range of investment assets that all work towards meeting one primary goal, which is to make money for the investor. One of the assets that is gaining ground is penny stocks. The name implies that you would be investing pennies, however, this is not entirely true.

Penny stocks are investments that are low in price. They may not be as low as a penny, but they are normally lower than $5. Their low values mean that they are not as popular as traditional stocks, yet, they can still give one a handsome return. The reason that many people tend to stay away from penny stocks is because they have been tainted over time with numerous scams and elevated levels of corruption.

There is a simple way to avoid the scams which could cost you your investment. Before you choose penny stocking, you need to choose a high quality company to invest in. This company will have clear competitive advantages, revenue that is on the increase, a growing market share, barriers of entry that are high for their sector as well as strong fundamentals. To select the right company is no small feat, so you need to find a professional penny stock analyst for help.

Here are some reasons why penny stocks are considered highly risky and cause concern for investors:

1. There is little information that is availed to the public about these stocks. Investors need to have sufficient information pertaining to every stock that they want to trade in but penny stocks are different. Not many people know much about these kinds of stocks and so, there is no sufficient information that can be used to guide the investors in making the right decisions. The little information that is available to the public cannot be fully trusted because it is not really from credible sources.

2. Companies selling penny stocks often do not have any history: most of these companies are newly established and so, they do not have a past that investors can check out to determine if they are good enough to invest in or not. Some of these companies are those that are approaching bankruptcy and they are looking for some financial support in order to stay in operation a little longer. It is pretty hard to determine the stability of such stocks because they do not have any reliable history or they already have a bad reputation.

3. There are no standards in trading penny stocks: most of the credible stocks that are traded in the common stock exchanges have minimum standards that are used to govern them and ensure that investors are getting something at the end of the day, not just the companies. This is not the case with penny stocks. Companies do not have to meet certain requirements in order to stay in the stock exchange and are able to move freely from one small exchange to the other without any issues at all. Investors are therefore risking so much investing in stocks that are not governed by any standards at all.

4. Lack of liquidity: Penny stocks are the kinds of stocks that do not have much liquidity and this means that they have high chances of not selling again. What business people do at that instant is to lower their prices so that they can seem attractive to some buyers. That is why penny stocks can be manipulated so much in order to benefit a few traders. Wise traders will buy as many stocks when the prices are low only to sell to other investors after a slight increase in the price, for a good return.

Understanding the Key Terms

Once you have received advice from your penny stock analyst, you will be ready to try your hand at trading, though you must be able to understand the terms that you are used. Here are the most common ones: -

- OTCBB – This stands for Over the Counter Bulletin Board. This is an exchange where you can trade stocks that have failed to meet the listing requirements of the main exchanges. Companies that trade their stocks in this exchange are usually the small businesses whose future growth cannot be guaranteed that is why investing in these business is considered as highly risky.

- Pink Sheets – Over the counter stocks which are not listed on exchanges that are established, such as NASDAQ or the New York Stock Exchange. This is another way through which stocks that do not meet the listing requirements of the main exchanges are traded. The pink sheets do not have any regulations at all.

- Bid – This is the price that you are able to sell your penny stocks shares.

- Ask – This is the price that you are able to buy your penny stocks shares.

- Stop Loss Percentage – This is the highest percentage level that you are willing to risk for a loss

- Profit Percentage Gain – This is the highest percentage level that you are willing to take for your profits.

- Pump and Dump – This is a strategy that is when trading in penny stocks which someone promotes a stock so that the price can increase and they are able to sell their stock at the higher price.

- DTCC: this stands for Depository trust and clearing Corporation. This is the corporation that handles the clearing securities of brokers. It is the body that ensures that brokers are offering the right services at all times, without scamming investors. When you decide to start investing with the help of a brokerage account, you have to ensure that the broker of your choice is DTCC eligible. This way, you will not be highly charged and also, you will have an easier time selling the penny stocks that you will invest in.

The Right Tools and Important Starter Tips

In order for you to be successful at penny trading, you need to have the right tools available at your disposal. To begin with, you must have a computer that is fast as well as reliable. Things change within seconds with penny stocks, and you do not want to miss out on a profit making opportunity. This means that your internet connection should also be fast, with minimal time loading pages and confirming transactions.

While ensuring you have this basic tools, you must pay attention to your security and safety as well. When carrying out financial transactions, ensure that you have a strong password. Avoid day trading while you are on a public connection, and if you have no choice, make sure that you log out of your account as soon as you are done.

As you are preparing your money for the trade, you should deposit it into your account a few days before you will need it. This is because money often takes a few days to reflect in your account, and to be available for purchasing stock.

Finally, when you are choosing your broker, you will likely select an online broker that handles a host of different assets. You need to confirm whether this broker is friendly towards penny stocks, and if there will be additional fees which are placed on the minimum deposits when trading penny stocks.

Penny stocks can make you a great return, and you should also be aware that they can cost you significant losses as well. Before you move forward, keep in mind the fact that penny stocks are high risk.

The penny stock market is highly volatile as even any negativity or hype around a penny stock can radically shift the share price.

For the most part, they are not regulated, which means that if something goes wrong, there is no safety net that will save you. This is also a positive, as it means you can benefit if things go right. To protect your money, you should do some research and establish which sights have received warnings from the regulators, and how much information the site is willing to disclose to an investor. With sufficient due diligence, you will be able to select a site for penny stock trading, knowing that you are making a calculated risk that could have a fantastic payoff.

Although penny stocking is seen to be a form of investment, it is more like a game. When you play a game you have a winner, a loser and a game plan. In order to get to the win, you evaluate every scenario and make calculated decisions. If you make a mistake, you accept that this could cost you the win. What this means is that at any time, the direction that you are taking in this game can change, and even with a loss on the way, you still have the room to make a comeback.

CHAPTER 7

Penny Stock Brokers

Penny stock brokers are very important in the trading business. They are particularly crucial to traders who are just getting started. Due to the rarity of trading in penny stocks, there are few people who know all about them, therefore, a trader can show you around the trade easily to help you get started with little or no issues at all. Penny stock brokers provide the trading platforms and infrastructure that investors use in their trading. In one way or another, you will need their help in trying to understand the trading platform well and maybe in making major trading decisions in your first days of trading.

Stock brokers can also influence the way that you trade in a major way. They can recommend a certain stock for instance, influence your trading behaviour and patterns and also help you with your sales to ensure that you are making the right move at the right time. Generally speaking, they are very important therefore you will need access to advice from a good broker by your side once you start trading in penny stocks.

Considering that penny stocks are associated with high risks, you have to choose a penny stock broker with a lot of care. The right broker will be of great help and he will ensure that you are not losing more than you should in those days that the trade goes against your expectations. Check out the reliability of a stock broker as well, to ensure that you can always count on his help and support when you really need it. There are certain criteria that you can use in order to ensure that you are making the right choice of a penny stock broker, including the following:

1. **The kind of trading platform the broker is offering**: Online trading is increasing in popularity these days. Therefore, it is possible that you will seek this platform for its consummate simplicity and the fact that you can monitor your trades any time with ease. Another thing that makes some brokers better than others are fast and safe mobile trading applications. This is what will ensure that you can trade even when you are on the go, as well as get information on what is happening with your trades in real time, all the time. The safety of these applicants has to be considered as well so that you will be sure that the money that you deposit in your account is safe and that you are the only one that is accessing your account at any given time.

   The traditional facilities that were mainly based on calls and pulls have no place in the current trading for penny stocks as modern day traders are online most of the time and they want to see what is happening in real time for better decision making.

   Prices fluctuate every minute when it comes to penny stocks therefore you need to be sure that you are monitoring the fluctuations as well so as not to miss out on a chance to make a profitable move.

Another thing that should be noted is that online platforms have self-help options that can reduce your trading costs considerably. There is information available all the time to help you keep up with the price changes so as to be able to make a quick decision when a chance presents itself.

2. **The charges**: The charges are very important in any part of stock trading. In penny stock trading, this should matter even more because every change in penny stock price will be charged. You are trading in the smallest amounts, and the profit that you make will also come in small amounts. You have to ensure that you are choosing a penny stock broker wisely so that you will not be charged more than you should. The profits that you will enjoy in the end will be determined by the charges that you incur whenever you buy or sell a penny stock, and you do not want the profit to be completely swallowed up.

Many investors make mistakes in choosing the wrong brokers and they end up diverting all their profits to their brokers. With penny stocks, you are already dealing with high risks. It will be too much to have to deal with high broker charges as well. When it comes to such high risk investments, it is good to determine beforehand how much you are willing to pay to the broker, then you can pick out a broker that matches your expectations.

Here are some of the charges that you should always be aware of:

- Transaction charges: This is the general charge that the brokers list on their websites and the charges are always levied per trade. Always look out for additional charges on the terms and conditions so as to be sure that you will only pay what the broker has stated and nothing more, even after some time of trading. This means that you need to take the time to read the small print, no matter how much it may seem to be. Some brokers are very cunning and they will charge a certain amount of money after you have made a certain number of trades. Have the right information at hand before you can sign or authorise any agreement.

- Charges on minimum brokerage per share: These are charges that will increase the amount of money that you will be paying to your brokerage. You have to check whether your preferred broker has a minimum brokerage on a per share charge, and check out the percentage in order to see roughly how much more you will be paying for the number of shares you intend to invest in. if such charges are there, you have to ensure that you invest in penny stocks whose prices will shoot up significantly otherwise you may not be able to cater for the broker charges and still enjoy profits in the end.

- The costs of operating a brokerage account: every penny stock trading account needs a maintenance fee that is charged annually. Some brokers will have other charges for depositing, money transfers and other charges that you should be aware of as all these will be affecting your profits so much. There could be withdrawal charges as well, when you are transferring money from your trading account.

- Charges on the minimum brokerage per order: Many brokers charge a minimum charge per trade and these charges are also meant to increase the amount of money that you will be paying to invest in the end. You need to be aware of these charges as well and ensure that the charges are agreeable with you before you sign up with the stock broker. With all these charges, the buying price will end up increasing and this means that you have to sell at a high price in order to be able to recover the money you have invested in the penny stocks and at least get some profits.

- The frequency of trading: Some brokers impose a minimum trade per month and if you want to trade more than the imposed number of trades, you might have to pay for it.

- Large Order Surcharges: There are some brokers who will charge you an additional amount of money for a large purchase. You need to be aware of this beforehand as well so that you will know when you will be required to pay more to invest more money in penny stocks. There are top up charges as well that will be charged when you want to add more shares of a certain company to what you already have.

- The minimum deposit: Many accounts have minimum account deposits that should sit in the account at all times, whether you are trading or not. If you take a longer time to start trading, you might be charged an inactivity fee as well.

3. **Depot and Nostro facilities**: Penny stock investors need to find out if their preferred stock broker offers both depot and nostro facilities. Depot or depository is your dematerialized account where you will be keeping all your shares. Nostro is like your bank account where all your money for buying and selling of shares will be kept. All brokers offer the depot account but only a few offer nostro account. A stock broker offering both the accounts will be the best one to choose because you need an instant and reliable money transfer facility at all times because of the instant changes in price of penny stocks.

4. **Response time**: A penny stock investor should always work with a broker that they can fully rely on and their response time on their website as well as the time they take to respond to phone calls should matter so much. You need a broker that will respond really fast so that you can easily get in or out of position immediately a chance presents itself. With the high volatility of penny stocks, you cannot afford any kinds of delays because you can lose so much money in a very short period of time.

5. **The tools and the functionalities offered**: Different broker's offers different tools and functionalities through their trading platforms in order to make trading easy for investors. If you want to access a broad range of customer care services, you

will choose a broker that offers just that. You have to be sure that you will not be paying for some of these tools and functionalities though because some promotions do not specify on such matters. If they are charged, you will just choose features that you really need to cut down on the trading costs.

CHAPTER 8

Finding the Best Penny Stock Investments

Looking for penny stocks is not the same as looking for your typical stocks, as companies that sell their stocks on the stock market tend to be quite large, where as those that sell penny stocks are much smaller. This means that they are largely ignored by financial analysts and therefore there is minimal information online.

As mentioned earlier, the easiest way that you can find a penny stock investment is through your broker. Since these statements are so high risk, you need to know how to double check any information you have been given, so that the penny stock that you agree to trade in will be profitable for you.

Sometimes, finding a broker that is willing to trade in penny stocks can be a challenge, as they small investment may not translate into a return that the broker finds worthwhile. Therefore, you need to be familiar with over the counter trading, where the buyer and the seller have to deal directly with each other.

To ensure that you choose the right penny stocks, you can be guided with the following strategies: -

Stability

The company that you choose to purchase penny stocks from needs to be stable so that you can trust that you will not lose your investment. Make sure that it is profitable, and not just breaking even or making a loss. When it cannot manage its own funds, do not imagine that your investment will be well managed so that you get a return. This means that it should have enough funds to pay off all of its creditors, without having to close the business. In addition, a strategic plan for the future where the company gets listed on a major exchange reveals that a good direction is being followed, and you are more likely to benefit from a return.

The Next Best Thing

When you are purchasing penny stocks, you may be tempted to buy into the next big thing. If a stock promises to have cutting edge bio-technology and create a drug that will change the world, you may want to get on the bandwagon before everyone else so that you can make a profit when it goes nuclear. Don't!! Just don't!! Avoid being trapped in the buzz and excitement of stocks that have no track record. To find the best penny stock investments, you should find a track record that reveals the stock is successful. This could be in the form of earnings on a quarterly basis, or tracking of sales – anything that can be verified in numbers. Sure things, tips or rumours will lead you down towards losing your investment and should be ignored completely.

The Pink Sheet Penny Stocks

You should always look for penny stocks that are in some way regulated and follow certain rules, and those that are on pink sheets do not. They are not required to file financial statements on a regular basis and quite often, do not met the listing requirements that are given for exchanges. The penny stocks that appear on the exchange are a better bet, although it may take some time to find them. These are able to meet minimum risk standards and therefore, will make better and safer penny stock investments.

Share Volumes

A company that has penny stocks should be trading at least 100,000 shares being traded on a daily basis. This reveals a consistency and ability to stay relevant in the market. If the amount that is being traded falls below this number, or you cannot find information on the trading volume, then you will be taking an uninformed risk which could result in the loss of your investment. Furthermore, if may become a challenge to sell your shares after you have purchase them, even though their prices are on the rise.

Do not be tempted to trade shares whose value falls below 50 cents for each share. This is because they lack liquidity, and the end result will not be worthwhile. Remember that the share volumes should be consistent on a day to day basis, where you allow for differences of plus or minus twenty percent. Large swings in volume from one day to the next is not a reassuring sign.

Price Purchase

Penny trading is not normally carried out with a pre-determined price. When you want to purchase penny stocks, there will be numerous sellers in the market and you will select your stock based on the prices that they give you. You need to make your purchase based on the ask price, making sure it is the lowest one that you can find for a particular stock. You will then sell it at the highest bid price that you are able to find. This is how you will make a profit easily.

When looking for penny stocks to trade in, be careful about where you source your information. There are typical sources on information that will mislead you. To begin with free stock reports are not advised, as they are often skewed towards benefiting a particular penny stock rather than helping you get a return. This also applies for emails that you receive as newsletters which are meant to give you the 'inside scoop' on the latest penny stock trades. Detailed research is the best way that you can be sure to make a wise decision. There are no short-cuts.

Researching Penny Stocks

Finding the best stocks to invest in will start with some research on what is available in the market. Today, finding penny stocks that you can invest in is very easy, all thanks to the internet. However, you have to narrow down your options to the best so as to minimize the risks and maximize your returns thereafter. Here are some strategies that can help you determine if a certain stock is the right one or not:

i) Check out the company data: With the strategies above, you will have a list of companies that you can invest in. there are so many new and developing companies that you can consider investing in but you have to be sure that the companies have just what you are looking for That is why you have to go through each of the company's data to know more about its operations and future plans. This is the only way you can tell if a business is worth your investment or not. From the company's data, you can easily tell if a company has plans for future growth and the chances it has to achieve just that. Avoid companies that will not present any viable data about themselves as this could mean that they have so much to hide.

ii) Analyse the balance sheets: a balance sheet has vital information pertaining to the company that you want to invest in, information that can interest you so much. It for instance has a list of all the assets that the company owns, the receivables, properties and other investments. The balance sheet will also show you the amount of money that the company owes other companies as liabilities. Basically, the balance sheet will show you how solid a certain company is, so that you can make an informed decision thereafter. You need to be sure that the company that you will invest in is able to deal with all its debts especially the short term liabilities.

iii)   Determine the profitability level of the company: What you need for this is the company's statement of earnings or the company income statement. This statement will show you how much the company has been bringing in as revenue over a certain period of time as well as how much money out of this revenue the company has spent in its expenses. You need to ensure that the company you are interested in has brought in more than it spent on the expenses, which is called a positive operating income. Note that companies that operate at losses are less likely to improve in the coming years, therefore it will be a bad idea to consider investing in those.

iv)   Check out the company's cash flow: There are company cash flow statements that will show you where the business got its cash from and how the cash was spent. These statements will show you the kind of business you are about to invest in. You can for instance tell what the company does with its cash, whether it uses the cash to expand its operations, to run its operations, to clear its debts among other things. These can easily tell you if the business has potential to grow or not and this is the point where you make the decision to invest or not to invest. A company that is always struggling to pay off debts is not stable enough but one that is investing and paying for its operations has great potential for growth.

v) Talk to the experts: There are financial experts that can help you make the right decision when you are investing in penny stocks. Experts from the company should not convince you about anything at all because those are paid by the company to lure you to their stocks. Choose different financial experts and listen keenly to their perspective. There are internet sites as well, that can help you get information that will make decision making easier for you. These mainly deal with business and financial issues and they always have up to date information to help you know the real matters at that particular time. There are experts who are always conducting their research about the developing companies and they write exclusive reports about these companies. You need to read such reports to make an informed choice. If they say something that you do not want to hear, this does not mean that they lack understanding in what you are looking to achieve. It simply means that you need to do even more research to determine whether they are right or not.

vi) Be aware of scams: Penny stock scams exist and investors need to know about these so that you will devise ways through which you can avoid falling on their traps. Some illegal businesses will use the names of businesses that do not even operate in order to sell their stocks and make some money. You end up investing in a business that is either not legal or one that does not even exist. Try to avoid buying stocks from companies that will solicit you to buy their stocks. To be on the safe side, only buy stocks from companies that you have personally researched on, and those whose information you trust fully. Losing money in penny stock investments is very easy that is why investors have to take time to be sure about the investment first.

CHAPTER 9

The Secrets to Making Profit

Penny stock trading is undoubtedly high risk, which gives it the benefit of being high profit as well. However, you will not make a profit without a few essential tips to help you along. If you are used to trading normal stocks and bonds, you will find that the strategies you employ in those markets, will not give you the best results with penny stocks. You need a new set of skills. You need to change your perspective towards making profit. Here is what you should look for.

Financials

This has been mentioned in research, though it is so crucial that it is worth emphasising so that it remains top of mind for any potential penny stocks trader or investor. Before you would make any investment in a company, you would typically check to see their financial standing, as this will play a part in whether you get your desired return. The same applies when you are looking to invest in penny stocks. Find out about the financial statements for the company that you are looking to invest in and go through them in detail. They should be current, and if possible, you should look at the statements for the past three years so that you can identify any patterns. If the penny stock that you want to invest in is from a company that does not have financial statements, or those which are available are of questionable quality, then you should not invest in these stocks as you will not make a profit.

Underlying Business

This ties in to growth within a sector or an industry which will determine whether purchasing a specific penny stock is a good idea. As penny stocks are high risk and fraught with corruption, it is possible that you will come across a shell company. This is a company that simply exists on paper, and does not have any real business operations. When dealing with shell companies, you will notice a high volatility in the shares as they are pumped into the market to feed in to high demand from potential investors, and then they are dumped, bringing down the price substantially and leaving you at a loss. If you are keen on making a profit, you must find a company which is real with business operations that you are able to verify.

To get this information, you can check sites like Yahoo Finance and Google Finance as these will also include news about your chosen penny stock. If nothing comes up, then it is an indication that you are not choosing the right company. The OTCBB is also an excellent source of information for the penny stock market.

Play the Pump and Dump

The penny stocks that you are trading may be from a legitimate source, yet even then, the pump and dump strategy may be used by someone who is looking to make a profit. If you find yourself caught up in this scenario, you should not panic. Instead, you can strategize so that you create an excellent profit for yourself. They key to making a profit here is knowing when you should sell, by being able to identify the patterns in trading.

Profit Percentage Gain

Put a cap on the amount of profit that you are willing to get from each trade, and resist the urge to get greedy. Greed is the reason that many penny stock traders make massive losses, as they want to keep pushing their returns in the hope that they will gain more. When you are on the rise, the moment that the trade reaches the profit percentage gain that you had established for yourself, you should pull out., This gives you the room to decide whether you want to re-invest in that penny stock or move on to a different option.

Turnaround Companies

These are companies that have gone through bankruptcy and are now coming up again. They may be going through a period of restructuring and have the backing of excellent investors. This means that during the restructuring process, the shares that they sell will be cheap, qualifying as penny stocks. Nonetheless, they are only moving in one direction and that is up, therefore as they increase in their success, the value of their stock is also expected to go up. This means that you will make a sure profit.

Pay Attention

If you want to consistently make profit, the main secret is that there is no short cut. You need to commit your time and energy to the process. One way is to always pay attention. This calls for you to pay attention to what is happening with the price of your stock, possibly taking an entire day to evaluate its movement. Doing this will make it easier for you to determine the patterns of increase and decrease in value that it has. This will make it easier for you to know when you should buy or sell.

While you are paying attention, do not lose sight of what penny stocks really are. These are short term investments and they are not suited to changing your financial future. This is because they are speculative in nature. If you make the right decisions through well thought out strategies, great – you make a profit. They should make up only a small section of your portfolio and should not be your entire portfolio.

CHAPTER 10

Making Use of Trend Stocks

Jumping on the bandwagon of an upward trend can help you to make a profit when you are trading in penny stocks. To benefit from these, you must be able to identify a trend. This is what happens when a stock in a specific sector shows consistent gains over the period of a day or more than one day. These gains need to be significant, often reaching the 100% mark. There trends will often happen when there is something that is changing within the sector that the penny stock is on.

This means that you need to pay attention to what is happening on the ground, in an economical point of view. There may be a new product launching, an advancement in the sector or any event that will have a trickle-down effect on financial markets. These markets are not limited to the penny stock trading market, but also include the stock exchange. When it appears that something is happening in this way, as a trader, you should begin to buy up as much penny stocks that you can, with the plan to sell them in the short run to realise a good profit.

An interesting way that you can identify a trend stock is by following press releases. These will often give insight on the direction of a company, and this affect the price of the penny stocks. Consider this example: -

Technology giant Microsoft announces that they are diversifying their business and will begin offering special day packages through authorised dealers for their latest projects. This is so that they are always in tune with customer needs and demands. They also explain that this move is expected to bring in billions of dollars in revenue on an annual basis.

Several smaller companies that trade in penny stocks provide press releases explaining that they will be amongst the authorised dealers that will be working with Microsoft. Within a very short period, the price of the penny stocks in these companies is likely to grow substantially as the understanding from traders will be they are about to capitalise on a multi-billion-dollar opportunity. Before the heat from the announcement dies down, there is an excellent chance to make a significant profit by selling when the demand is high. However, this is only possible if a purchase of the stock was made before the big jump in price.

When trading in penny stocks, paying attention to trends is an excellent way for you to make a large amount of money in a short amount of time. The returns can be truly astronomical, reaching upwards of 1000%. You need to be careful though not to be overtaken by temptation and greed, and choose for yourself an appropriate profit percentage gain. If things change for any reason, this will ensure you do not make a massive loss. Penny stocks are speculative in nature, so anything can happen. This type of increase is known as value is called a rocket stock.

Staying Up to Date

The above example is an instance where you are paying attention to what is happening in a select industry so that you can capitalise on it. Penny stocks cover a range of industries, therefore, if you want to take advantage of trends to make money, you must be up to date with your current affairs. This means that you spend time each day reading and watching the news so that you know what is happening in the world. When you hear that a particular sector is about to experience change, invest in penny stocks in that sector. You will now find trends on a daily basis, however, by understanding what is happening in sectors, you should be able to identify trends every two or so months.

When there are many buyers for a specific stock, do not be discouraged. With penny stocks this is when you should be making a purchase so that you can ride the wave all the way to profit. You simply way for the price to increase slightly and then sell. Do not become attached to your stock in the hope that it is your financial salvation. Focus on capping a certain amount of profit.

Cyclical Trends

In addition to the trend that has been described, there are cyclical trends that can occur as well. The only way you can tell that a penny stock has a cyclical trend is by paying attention to the patterns of the stock. Cycles only remain for limited periods of time and are based on external variables in the trading environment. An analysis of the health of the company can help you to identify a certain cycle. For example, a manufacturing company may have an increase in their penny stock price around holiday times when there is a spike in their sales. Following this period, the price returns to normal. This means that as a trader, you have the change to make a profit while the price is increasing before the holiday.

The profit that you can make from this trend may not reach the 1000% that is possible with the rocket trend, though you can count on making a consistent profit for a few weeks, perhaps up to 20%, when you are taking advantage of a cyclical trend.

Trading in trend stocks can be risky, especially if you miscalculate the trend and therefore put in too much of an investment at the end. The way to profit is preparation. Know what is happening on the ground and learn how to stay abreast of financial statements so that you can easily identify trends. If you have, you will find that this is a sure win strategy that can significantly increase any returns that you make with penny stock trading.

CHAPTER 11

Trading Penny Stocks

High risk investments are a preference of many stock traders because of the expected high returns if things work out well as per your plan. Investing in penny stocks entails investing in stocks of small businesses that have a high potential for growth. There is usually no guarantee that these businesses will do well in the market but in the event that they do, the investor stands to benefit a lot from it. Penny stocks are highly risky because such small companies can collapse any minute and this means that you could lose all the money that you have invested in it.

Trading in penny stocks is therefore a serious affair that need to be well thought of before one puts their money into the investment. If you have already studied them well and you have made up your mind, it is time to start trading.

Develop your trading strategy

Success in stock trading is mainly determined by the stock trading strategy one uses and this is not exceptional for penny stock trading. You need a penny stock investing strategy that you will stick to the end in order to meet all your trading goals in the end. You have to always be prepared to face risks in this kind of trade. Many penny stocks have been branded unworthy of investing by expert traders, therefore you should know from the beginning what you are up against. The fact of the matter is that only a small percentage of all penny stocks can guarantee a good return for investors.

The kind of strategy that you will use in trading will be determined by a number of factors:

Your investing needs

Due to their high risks, penny stocks are not suitable for long term investors. If you have long term savings plans, it will not be advisable to invest in such kinds of stocks. The risk of loss is quite high and if you are saving for the future then you could end up losing so much money in a matter of minutes. If you have short term investment needs on the other hand, you will do so well in penny stock investing. Such kinds of stocks are good for investors who prefer to buy and sell frequently.

Your constraints

There are certain constraints that are really hard to negotiate and investors must consider them as well in determining the way that they will trade in penny stocks. If for instance there are certain stocks of a certain company that you cannot invest in, you need to choose a trading strategy that will not compromise on that. Some investors or traders have inherited some stocks as well and they will not let those go for personal reasons. You need to be aware of all this so as to know where to start trading.

Your risk tolerance

Just like in all the other kinds of stocks, there are penny stocks that are more risky than the others. There are those stocks that have high trading volumes and this makes them better than those that have low trading volumes. You have to be wise in your choice. In order to balance the amount of risk that you can take with the kind of returns that you are expecting. Ask yourself how far you are willing to go just so that you can get the kind of returns that you are eying from that investment. This should guide you on the kind of strategy you should trade with.

Your return expectations

Every investor has some kind of expectation on every investment that they make. The kind of return that you are expecting from your stocks portfolio will guide you to the kind of strategy that is right for you. People differ so much in what they require from their investments, that is why there are different strategies for different penny stocks investors. The kind of returns you want will also tell you how aggressive your trading strategies should be, because you have to meet your requirements in the end.

Always be ready for a loss

Penny stocks are very cheap when compared to the high value securities and the main reason why this is so is because there is always a high risk for loss. Many companies eventually fail and investors lose so much of their investments. Investors should always be aware of this so that in case it happens, they will not be affected so much. That is why it is good to diversify when you are investing in such stocks. Some businesses succeed in the end and this means that you can enjoy some good returns after all, but always be prepared for the worst to happen so that you will accept the outcome and move on with ease.

Purchasing Penny Stocks

Once you know the companies that you are going to invest in and you have your trading strategy well developed, it is time to make your first purchase. You will need an investment account for this. Register with a trading platform so that you can start making trades right away. You have to ensure that you are registering in a trading platform that will give you access to penny stocks though, since there are those that do not allow penny stock trading.

Beginners in stock trading will have to start here. Create an account and deposit some money into your account that will be used for your first penny stocks purchases. Cofounder the commission charges at all times, because there are trading platforms that will charge more than the others. You also need to consider your trading needs as well when choosing the right trading platform.

Traders who already have trading accounts for other stocks can use the same account to buy their penny stocks. You just have to check out the kind of plan you have signed for to see the kinds of charges you will face once you start trading in penny stocks.

Monitoring your investments

The value of penny stocks changes rapidly, so an investor has to be on the lookout at all times in order not to miss a chance to buy or sell their stocks. You need to monitor all the stocks that you have invested in closely at all times to know when to make a move. Always buy when the prices are low and sell immediately the prices go up so as not to miss the chance to sell at a profit.

You also need to keep a close eye on your portfolio's performance to know how well or even how badly you are doing every so often. This will motivate you to work harder especially if you are not doing so well already.

One thing that investors need to know is that they should maintain the same trading strategy throughout. Your trading strategy has been well developed, with great considerations, therefore changing it in the middle of trading just because you are not getting the expected returns is a bad idea. You have to be consistent in stock trading if you want to be a successful trader.

Keep investing. Penny stocks are not fully reliable; therefore, an investor should be ready to keep investing in order to enjoy some profits from them. Sometimes you will realize that some stocks are not doing so well and the only option you have at that point is to sell the off then buy those that you feel are doing better. Once you start trading, you will be able to see what is happening in the stock market clearly to be able to get serious in trading for the small profits.

CHAPTER 12

Penny Stock Trading Rules

With these strategies and secrets at your disposal, you can make some wise decisions when it comes to penny trading so that you attain a profit. You can also be further guided by some rules that will guarantee you keep your eye on the prize. There rules include the following: -

Make the Final Decision

Penny trading is different from typical trading where you give your money to a broker and trust their judgement to make a good trade for you. With this type of trading, you need to make your own decisions, and as much as you take advice from other people, do not be pressured into following that advice is it does not feel right. Trading costs money, and you should not be naïve about people who are willing to give you a free helping hand. Therefore, avoid the rumours and deals that are made in chat rooms or on message boards. Do your research on your own and in detail and then make your choice.

Same Day Trading

Penny stocks are speculative and meant to be short term investments. Do not hold onto them longer than necessary in the hope that they will change in their value. Usually, growth spurts occur on a daily basis so as much as possibly buy and sell on the same day.

This also helps to keep you liquid as when you deposit money in your account for trading, it may take several days to become available. In that period, you could lose out on the change to make a considerable profit. With daily trading, you will always have money that is available for a trade. Do not get too attached and take each day at a time.

Study the Market

In addition to staying abreast with news to do with money markets, you need to study the market on a daily basis. This is best done at the close of the market. You are doing this so that you can establish which of the stocks in a given day were performing well and which ones are not. Keep track of these in a journal. You will find that you can track percentage gains, and then back these up with information to understand why there are gains. This will help you know whether there is a trend stock that you can take advantage of. Dedicating thirty minutes at the end of each day is enough to ensure that you get the information you need.

Bid and Ask Gaps

To be able to control your money in penny stock trading, you must pay attention to the bid and ask gaps. When the gap is too large, for example, the bid price is $1 and the ask price is $2, when purchasing shares, you will need to spend $2. However, when selling shares, you will only get $1. This means that 50% of your investment will be lost. This puts you in a position where you must wait for the price to go up so that you can sell.

A tight gap between the bid and the ask is an excellent advantage so that you can control your funds. This limits the amount that you can lose and is an indication that there is a significant amount of volume being traded. This is an indication that the penny stock being traded is trustworthy.

CHAPTER 13

How to Get the Most Out of Penny Stocks

So many people are attracted to penny stock trading today because they do not cost much money and also because there are great chances of making huge returns from them. However, what many traders overlook is the possibility of losing so much money from penny stock investments. Traders with a good amount of money have a wide variety of options to choose from when it comes to investing but for someone with just a small amount of money, the choices are limited and this is where penny stock trading comes in. You have to ensure that you are trading safely at all times and this is the only way you can get the most out of your investment. Here are some key issues that will help you out:

1. Only focus on penny stocks with a high volume: Investors should be aware of the number of stocks traded in a day and the dollar volume as well. You are better off trading in stocks that sell a good number of shares in a day. A trading volume of about 100,000 shares in a day is a good sign. Trading in stocks that have a low trading volume is a bad idea as it becomes hard for one to get out of their trading position. Also, consider the stock price as this is what determines the liquidity of the shares. You want to invest in stocks that you can easily buy and sell as this is the only way you will make some money in the end, therefore watch out for what is best.

2. Do not dwell so much on the success stories: There are all kinds of penny stock success stories out there these days and these are used to lure investors to invest in stocks. These stores will be sent to your email, you will come across them in social media websites and anywhere else where business people are sure that potential investors will get to read them. This stories bring out only the good side of penny stocks while the bad side stays hidden. As you know, any kind of investment is full of risks and there are those investments that are risker than the others. Penny stocks are highly risky; therefore, you have to be careful before you can make the final decision.

    Experts will always advice investors to look at penny stocks as something that you cannot really trust. Also, take time to study the kind of stock that you want to invest in so as not to make regrettable mistakes.

3. Avoid falling for a certain stock: Companies want investors to fall in love with their stocks so that they will be compelled to invest in them. That is why they will use all kinds of stories to divert your attention to their stocks so that you will love them more. Do not allow people to compel you to invest in a certain stock. You have to do your own research first to find out how the stock is and how it has been doing in the past. Choose a stock to invest in according to your needs and investment goals. You will not go wrong if you make your own decisions.

4. Limit your share size: Many people invest so much money in a stock that they like the most without realizing that in case of

a risk, they stand to lose so much money in the end. There are those stocks that promise good returns and one may be compelled to invest more in them. However, always look at the worst side of every situation. What will happen if you want to get out quickly yet you have invested in so many shares? You might have to stick around for a longer time and this means that you will be losing so much in the end. With the swift nature of penny trading, this will clearly be counterproductive for you. Limiting your share size ensures that you are able to get out as quickly as possible when things start going south.

Also, do not trade large positions because you cannot tell for sure what will happen during the trading period. Position sizing is one thing that traders have to be very careful about. Trading large positions is a great risk that beginners should be careful about.

5. Always read disclaimers: All manner of tips will be sent your way by business people that wants to market their stocks to potential investors and all kinds of promises will be made. This is another area where potential investors fail terribly. Most of these people are paid to market the company, therefore you do not expect them to say anything bad about the business' stocks. You have to dig deeper yourself to know the other side of the stocks before you can finally make the decision. A business will always send you trading tips in order to make you think that it is the best one to invest in. This is always their target, but if you read the disclaimer and understand more about the

stocks, you should be able to make the right decision in the long run. Remember, the disclaimer is always there, but it is often written in the smallest possible font.

6. Never sell penny Stocks Short: Many people will think of shorting their pumped up penny stocks, but this s a wrong move. This is because of the volatility of penny stocks. If you make a mistake and you end up on the other side of the trade, you can lose so much, and this is something that you should avoid by all means. Another thing you should know about penny stocks is that finding penny stock shares that you can easily short can be difficult especially those that can guarantee you a good return. As a beginner, there are certain things that you just have to leave out for the trading experts.

7. Do not hold for long: The secret behind buying and holding is in order to make more returns than someone that buys and sells off quickly. This will not work very well for you if you invest in penny stocks. With penny stocks, you have to sell quickly for a small profit at a time because there is no guarantee that things will get better after sometime. One thing that you should know about penny stocks is that you can easily make a 30% profit or even a 20% profit after a few days. This is the time to sell, after a few days for something small, instead of waiting for a higher profit that may never come. If you want to trade safely in penny stocks, accept the small profit and move on. So many people lose because of being greedy.

8. Do not be too trusting: Companies use all manner of strategies in order to lure investors to invest in their stocks. If you want to be safe as you invest in penny stocks, do not be too trusting. First of all, do not listen to the company management. The company will do its best to convince you to go ahead with the investment even when it is not god enough. The intention of many companies is just to get some money to be able to stay in operation and this means that they can create ghost penny stocks in order to raise the amount of money that they require. You have to be careful not to fall into such traps.

CHAPTER 14

Penny Stock Scams

Investors should always be aware that anything which offers high returns at a small cost can be highly risky and these are the kinds of investments one should think carefully about before they can invest a lot of money into them. Even after companies were asked to register under such bodies as OTC in order to always provide reports pertaining to their operations, penny stock scams are still on the high side and many investors are losing so much money to these scams. It is for this reason that many people are wary of investing in penny stocks, and believe them to not be real. Investors do not have to lose their hard earned cash to scams, especially now that there is information all over the internet about these scams and how one can avoid falling into the traps.

There are certain red flags that you can look out for when you are looking for penny stocks too invest in, so as to at least avoid falling into traps set by scammers:

- So many promotions that do not really look official. Scammers will do their best to look official and genuine therefore you have to be careful not to be lured by these promotions. Most of these promotions come through the internet and others through emails. Take time to find out if the information you just read is true. In addition, human beings are perceptive. When you are looking at a scam message, you may believe that something is not quite right, but find it difficult to point out exactly what the problem could be. Trust your instincts.

- Telemarketing calls. These are very common these days but one thing that potential investors should know is that telemarketers will not give you full information and they will always cover up any negative information that can make you suspect a raw deal. Their job is to wear you down with conversation until you give in and invest.

- Any claims that you hear about pertaining to insider information that makes penny stocks look as if they are the next big thing. They have been there for a while, so do not believe that they are a new discovery that will change your life.

- Newsletters and online forums that come with a fake label yet they have so many recommendations.

- Too good to be true offers.

How to avoid some of these scams

1. Always conduct due diligence: The problem with many investors is that they do not take enough time too research about a stock that they intend to buy without buying it. This is risky for all kinds of stocks and it is riskier for penny stocks because they are already highly risky stocks. The rush to buy stocks because you do not want their prices to go up before you invest in them should end if you do not want to make a regrettable

and costly mistake. Do not allow someone else to tell you how great a certain stock is as well, when you can easily find that out for yourself. Spend only a few hours researching about a certain stock and you can save yourself from a huge mess that can cost you a lot of money in the end.

2. Always seek for sufficient information: A smart investor is a well-informed investor. As they say, information is power and this can make a huge difference in the way that you invest and the kinds of returns you are getting. Do not be the kind of investor that is easily attracted by the stock price. As mentioned in the earlier chapters, you have to look deep into the company to determine if it is worth of your investment or not. Gain access into its financial records and look out for stock market capitalization as well. Stock market capitalization can easily tell you the kind of value the stock has. Good thing is that these days there is so much information that you can count on in order to make the right decisions. Many companies will not be willing to provide their information especially if they have something to hide from investors. Move on and look for another potential business if you come across one of these.

3. Marketing traps: Most of these scams come through marketing and promotions. Thanks to the advancing technology, many marketers today are able to create promotes that can easily lure investors and this is where investors fall. Social media promotions can easily carry a lot of false information and since so many people are using these platforms, you can imagine just

how many people can be convinced to invest in penny stocks that are just a scam. These promotions are quite tempting and some of them offer tips that seem irresistible to many potential investors. You have to be careful with these as they could be scams. No real trader will tell you all of their secrets so that you can make a quick return – they will be too busy making a profit for themselves.

4. Misleading information in news: There are so many writers that are paid to promote a certain company or promoter and you will quickly believe what they are saying just because they claim to have done research on the said company. These are some of the things that are happening on all platforms today. These people will be paid to provide false information in the news just so that they can hype a certain promoter or company. What you learn about the stocks in the end is totally different from what the promoter was saying.

Conclusion

Penny stock trading is different from traditional trading as you will be using lower amounts of money due to the low share prices. However, there is the chance to make some significant returns, if you have the right strategies in place.

This book has outlined for you some key secrets to making a profit, and the strategies that you can use as a beginner to make money.

Exercise your wisdom and knowledge when you are looking for the right penny stocks to invest in. As the market is swamped with scam artists and corrupt people, it is better for you to do your own research and establish which the right stocks are for you. It is best for you to take some time to perfect this before you begin actual trading, so that you know how to identify stocks, how to read the market and where you are likely to make a profit.

When on a trading site, take some time to practice using a demo account if there is one available. This will help you establish your own style as a penny stock trader, and also, you will understand when you should buy and sell your stock for profit.

Finally, an excellent way to guarantee that you get a return with penny stock trading is to make use of trend stocks as a strategy. If you study them well, and learn to identify patterns, you will be able to make returns up to 1000% of your investment in a short period of time. This is why penny stock trading is so exciting.

Take it one day at a time, do not worry about making mistakes and learn along the way. Penny stock trading could make you a pretty penny if done the right way.

Day Trading
For Beginners
2nd Edition

Day Trading Basics

Do's and Don'ts

And the Small Letters

Contents

Introduction

Day trading is not a new concept, and has been around since the early 1990's though it is only now that it is becoming really popular with the general population. The simplest way to describe day trading is the practice of trading in stocks on whatever stock exchange within the same trading day. Strictly speaking day traders have to have closed all their positions by the end of the trading day.

Day trading is a high risk business. As a day trader, the chances of you making a loss are much higher than those of someone who trades on the stock market for the long term. As all the money traders make for the day needs to be made in roughly 8 to 12 hours, this can make day trading become a challenge even for seasoned investor.

Though there are many ways to look at day trading, whether you focus on price momentum, trade patterns or a whole host of different strategies, there is one thing that all day traders have in common. They all look for the highest profit margin possible, and for ways to meet their target for the day in the least time possible.

They are able to so adequately because of an understanding of what day trading entails. As a beginner looking to explore this field, it is imperative to understand that day trading is not something you can simply do as a hobby. It requires time, training, patience and understanding. It should be approached as a profession.

If you want to find out what it entails, how to get started, and even understand what you need to set yourself up, then this is the right book for you. This book promises to introduce you to some of the strategies you need to follow to become a successful day trader, the pitfalls you may face, and the successes that you may encounter. It shall also teach you how to make the most of challenging situations when you are trading. So if you are ready to start your journey into the world of day trading, keep on reading. You will not be disappointed.

CHAPTER 1:

The History of Day Trading

In the beginning of financial trading, the most important US stocks were traded on the New York Stock Exchange or NYSE in a very long and tedious process. After being contacted by a trader, a stock broker would pass on the order to a specialist on the ground who would then have to match the seller's offer with another broker's request to buy shares. Once this match was made, a ticket was drawn up which actually signaled the completion of the transaction.

The commission charged on these transactions at the time was fixed at 1%, meaning that to make any profit on a sale a trader had to make more than 1% on every transaction. Though this may not sound like much, it is a lot when you start piling up the dollars and, for this reason, day trading was not profitable.

In 1975, however, the United States Securities and Exchange Commission (SEC) abolished the fixed deposit allowing for brokers to charge fluctuating interest rates. This was an important move as it was now more lucrative for traders to buy shares while brokers could reduce their commissions, attracting higher investments and, in the long run, making more profit.

This significant change in work ethic had a domino effect on the way traders and brokers did business. On top of the incentives provided by the brokers to entice traders to spend more, this move also meant that the brokers had to reduce their settlement period to fewer days to avoid the larger risks they may encounter.

In any financial trading, the settlement period is the time it takes for any securities that have been purchased to be paid for. In the case of stock market trading, in the past the settlement period could be as long as ten days. These days due to the changes in trade behaviors, day trading included, this settlement period has been shortened to just three days or T+3. This change has also reduced the risk of traders defaulting though this reduction in has also been helped by the advancement of technology.

The Evolution of Modern Day Trading

This technological evolution has been going on for the better part of 60 years, with one of the first and probably biggest advantages of this being Electronic Communication Networks (ECNs). ECNs are primarily large computer-based networks where brokers and traders alike can post their securities or stocks for a certain price (called the 'ask') and other traders and brokers can the offer to buy the stocks at a certain price (called the 'bid').

The first ECN was called 'Instinet' now 'Inet' and it was created in 1969. Its primary mandate was to provide a safe, secure way for major financial institutions to bypass traditional stock exchanges such as the NYSE, making it easier and more convenient to trade insecurities. It also significantly brought down the price of trading and allowed for trade to continue even after the markets had closed for the day.

In the beginning, these ECNs were not geared towards medium and small investors, with some people even calling hostile towards this demographic. This was because they favored large institutions, giving them better prices and, therefore, better returns on investments.

CHAPTER 2:

Day Trading and the Stock Market

In 1971 the National Association of Securities Dealers (NASD) introduced the first ever fully electronic stock exchange in the world, the National Association of Securities Dealers Automated Quotations more commonly known as NASDAQ. Though it started off as a quotation system, the Nasdaq gained so much popularity that it inspired numerous changes in legislation and practices carried out at the time.

Practices that changed included moving away from paper share certificates, written share registers, use of the postal service, physical shipment and telex to more convenient electronic measures. NASDAQ also pioneered the development of real-time online systems rather than the old batch system.

Probably the biggest change and one that truly benefitted day traders was the changes in legislation that came about because of online trading and registration and the subsequent development of these electronic services. The most beneficial development was the creation of secure, cryptographic algorithms to safeguard the online transactions.

Introducing Market Makers

These changes helped to create 'Market makers' or the equivalent of the NYSE specialists. Market makers are firms that have inventory in stocks from various companies and are in the business of the buying and selling of those stocks online. Market makers sell their stock at a higher price than they would buy the same stock, creating what is referred to as a 'Spread' which is the difference between the asking and bidding figures.

Typically market makers do not care about the value of their shares, just that they sell them off at a higher price than the purchase price. For day traders, these market makers are an invaluable asset as they ensure that there is always an individual or firm willing to buy or sell you shares. At the moment, there are over 500 market makers operating on the NASDAQ.

To date perhaps the most significant impact on the development of day trading was the stock market crash of 1987. This crash opened up the door for the Small Order Execution System or SOES. This system was meant to facilitate low volume trades on NASDAQ meaning that all offers up to 1,000 shares had to be bought or sold immediately, at the sellers asking price. This led to a small group of traders who took advantage of this rule by buying and selling small orders to market makers, making enormous profits in the process.

Electronic Communications Networks and Day Trading

These trades were facilitated by ECNs, and not market makers. In the late 1990's some of these ECNs opened their doors to small investors and traders. Also New ECNs formed, driving competition through the roof and reducing commissions to an all-time low.

This combination of elements opened up the market for individual day traders. The low commissions allow for the individual day trader to purchase higher volumes of stock and make more trades in one day. The market maker in this case makes their money from high volume stocks such as Microsoft and Intel, which have small spreads, therefore allowing the market maker to make huge profits on a rise of just a few cents.

CHAPTER 3:

Day Trading Basics

As you prepare to plunge into day trading and start reaping profits, there are some basic facts that every new day trader needs to know. By understanding these facts, you will be able to dispel the myths about day trading so that you can operate in a successful manner.

To begin with, here is an explanation of what day trading is not. Day trading is not a high risk method of making money, where you will lose a lot more than you gain, especially in the short run. Neither is day trading a get rich quick scheme, where you can double your capital if it is sizeable enough – especially if you are hoping to do so within a month.

Day trading is often assumed to be simple, with a person sitting in front of their computer and playing with numbers. It is far from simple or easy, in fact, it requires training and strategy to get it right. Finally, day traders are not a bunch of kooky individuals who are their own brand of crazy. A day trader is someone like you, who has identified how to spot and capitalise on an opportunity.

Day Trading and Gambling

For a few years, day trading received a bad rap, particularly because it was being abused. Gamblers, for example, were looking to day trading in order to get their fix. When you consider the odds in gambling and those in day trading, you will be able to see the glaring differences.

In gambling, you are more likely to lose out, especially because the odds are never truly in your favour. With day trading, this is not the case. What is needed instead is proper planning, and one can be successful.

Beware of your Capital

In the process of game trading, you can end up with an unfortunate scenario. That is one where you lose everything, all the capital that you had invested. If you are looking for a way to grow your money and have placed your income into an account for day trading, you have made the wrong decision and could easily end up destitute. What one should do is dedicate some money to day trading, and then forget about it in terms of applicable use.

This does not refer to you using your discretionary income; it actually refers to your risk capital. Risk capital is simply money that you will not mourn over should you lose it. You should be able to afford it being gone.

Day Trading as Business

Should you have made the decision to go into the world of day trading, you need to realise that day trading is a profession or a career choice – it is not something that you do for fun on a Sunday afternoon as you would do with a hobby.

The reason is simple. Day trading requires an investment in time to learn how to get it right, and the development of skills. It also requires a detailed plan, and anyone who is looking to explore day trading as a hobby will likely lack the time to create a plan.

You may get Lucky

As a new trader, you may receive a visit from lady luck and make a significant amount of money from your very first trade. Though this can be fabulous for you, and will definitely build up your confidence, ensure that you continue to work for your future successes. If you are not careful, you may lose all your luck, (and your money) in your next trades.

If you did happen to be lucky, do not take it as a one off. Take the time to analyse and understand what exactly you did to cause such an incredible return. If you can retrace your steps, it makes it easier to apply this strategy to future trades, and hopefully maintain the same momentum.

Choosing a Market

Variety is the spice of life, and when you start day trading, it will appear that you are spoilt for choice. But even spices come with different heat meters, and you need to be careful to pick one that you can stand. This is the same with choosing a market. Here are some of the factors that you should consider.

- Whether you are in good financial health. This has a crucial role to play on the type of market that you will engage in.

- The strength of your personality and your custom trading system. The markets are a tough place to be, and if you do not have a thick skin, you may find that they can easily break you. You need to learn how to pick your battles so that you get closer to success.

- Your location geographically. You may find that you are limited to only a certain number or type of market.

When choosing market, you need to realise that as a newbie, you may be better suited for certain markets, while as an experienced day trader, and you may have enough skill to opt for something a little more risky. Beginning traders should begin by choosing a market that has minimal margin requirements, low tick values and is moving at a medium pace. This will ensure that you are not left hanging with nothing to show for your efforts.

Defining a Hot Tip

When it comes to day trading, there is quite an exchange of information, especially information that is meant to help with profitability. Most traders are privy to hot tips, which promise that if you follow them, you will make a killing. These types of tips are often communicated through the grapevine, and they can best be described as rumours.

The reason that they are so undercover in the way that they are passed on, and even from the person that is providing the information, it that in case of any problems, it is the trader who will be liable.

Should a day trader receive a hot tip which points towards some information that is legitimate, they would have an unfair advantage. This means that other people working in the same area could develop negative relationships or outlooks towards that particular day trader.

Insider Trading

Insider trading is slightly different from getting a hot tip though the way that the information is conveyed to employees is very similar. It is all about finding underground ways to pass the information forward. It is essentially any information that has not been made public, which can be used for the purpose of securing a sale. Insider training will usually be passed forward by a person whose opinion is prominent in a particular field, or who works within the field and has become aware of some new changes.

There are dangers for day traders who act on insider trading tips. These are usually penalties that are imposed should one be found with this information. If you were to profit from the insider trading information, then the penalty would be three times the amount of your profit, and if the government decides that as a trader, you were indulging in criminal behaviour, the penalty could be even higher.

The challenge with insider trading is that it is difficult to prove, as most of it happens with word of mouth, so there is no paper trail. In addition, a lot of the so-called tips that are given out as insider trading, often turn out to be completely baseless.

CHAPTER 4:

Day Trading Techniques

D ay Traders use a multitude of techniques to try and make a profit. Every single one of them is very useful to the average trader though it must be said that flexibility is the most successful strategy a day trader can use. This chapter seeks to outline some of these trading techniques and their relevance to day trading. Some of these techniques involve shorting stocks, instead of buying them, adding an increased risk factor to the transaction. Below are four of the most basic day trading techniques used by day traders everywhere.

1. Trend Following

Trend following is not a strategy used in day trading alone but in all forms of financial trading. It can be defined as the trading in securities and stocks not due to their market value, but due to the particular trends that have been affecting the market values over a set period of time.

In conventional trading circles, the trends can be followed over a period of days or weeks or even months to discern what the best investment would be. With day trading, however, the trend is followed over a much shorter term, a couple of hours at most.

A market 'trend' is the ability for a market price to move over time, whether it moves up or down. Most traders who practice trend following will study the market and wait for a trend to establish itself, and then depending on the nature of the trend, either buy or sell stocks on the market. Trend following is a good way to trade because it allows you the flexibility to decide for yourself whether the investment you are making is sound before diving into it.

Trends are affected by a number of different things, some of which prolong the current trend. For instance, some traders look for information that will confirm their beliefs about a particular trend. Confirmation bias like this has the power to keep the trend going, as once confirmation is found then the investor will apply it to that situation. Therefore, if the trend is negative, the investor will sell his shares to avoid making losses, continuing the negative trend for that particular stock listing.

Factors that have to be considered when trend following include, but are not limited to:

a) **Price:** This is by far the most important thing when it comes to trend following. Though other indicators may be used to forecast price fluctuations, only the actual price will give you an idea of how you need to interact with the market

b) **Risk Control:** Though completely eliminating losses is an impossible task, minimizing your losses should be paramount.

c) **Money Management:** These ties into risk control and are the decision of how much to invest in a trend. Too much and you risk losing more than you should, too little and you may not reap any benefits at all

d) **Rules:** Stick to the rules you laid out for yourself, trend following should be systematic.

e) **Diversity:** Recent research has shown that diversifying the assets that you follow is vital to professional trend followers.

2. News Playing

News playing is as the name suggests, playing the stock market depending on the news you have received for a particular security or stock on that market. If reports received state that a particular stock is doing well, then that would be a good reason to buy into it. Successful day traders are able to keep their emotions in check while news playing, as they know that emotion should not affect their final decision.

Once a particular news item has been released, it is important as a day trader to look at how this news is affecting the stock prices. As most news will be internally circulated before being released to the public, there may be a slight change in the share price just before any news is released. If there is a negative appreciation of the share price just before a news item is released, then it means that you need to sell your stock to avoid making losses. With day traders, it is said what is perceived is their reality while with conventional traders logic is relied on more.

For instance, when AOL and Time Warner joined forces just before the Dot-com bubble burst in the early 2000s, a day trader's profit margins were very high. Long-term investors at the time were not so lucky, as the merger seemed to have success written all over it, but three years down the road the investment would have proved to be a disaster. In the short term, the perception of the success of the merger was enough almost to guarantee a profit margin for day traders, but with the passage of time that opinion proved to be illogical and hence the losses made by long-term investors

3. Range Trading

Range trading or Range bound trading is a type of trade where a certain asset or stock is watched over a specified period of time. These stocks will have been rising and falling in value in an almost predictable pattern, with maximum and minimum values that can be pinpointed with relative ease and accuracy. The difference between the maximum and minimum values is called the 'range' or 'swing' of the stock value.

Range trading is often thought of in relation to trend following, but that is not the case, as with range trading unless there is an unexpected breakout in the range, the trend remains the same. Once a stock's range has been broken however, it is safe to assume that the trend that broke it be it a breakout (an increase in share price) or a breakdown (a decrease in share price), will continue for some time.

The best way to make money with range trading is to buy the stock when it's on its way back up the channel from its lowest point on the scale, then sell the shares when it reaches its peak. Some range traders even go to the extent of short-selling certain stocks as they know that a higher profit margin will be possible.

Mathematical algorithms in computer programs are often used to eliminate the human emotional factors that may affect a day traders decisions and are often written to give the trader buy and sell signals for selected securities.

Range trading is quite risky for all traders, long term investors and day traders alike, as the risk of making losses increases when trading in a range. A sideways price movement in the share price may also mean that no gains can be made on your investment. Worst of all, if there is an unexpected breakdown in the share prices, losses to you as a day trader can be enormous.

4. Scalping

Scalping is also referred to as spread trading and can be defined as the exploitation of the bid-ask spread by trading in securities rapidly over a very short period of time, usually minutes or even seconds. The theory most traders use when scalping is that if done properly, trading in stocks that make small increments in stock price are easier to catch than big ones.

Most scalpers will make between 10 and a couple of hundred transactions a day in the hope that they will make a profit. Scalpers have been compared to market makers as they help to maintain the liquidity of the market.

There are certain universal principles that all scalpers that trade on the markets are aware of. These are

a) The Lower Your Exposure, The Lower Your Risk

With scalpers holding stocks for just a few minutes on average, their exposure to those stocks is substantially reduced. This diminished time period means that there is a lesser chance of a scalper gaining huge losses due to changes in the stock price.

b) Small moves are easier to obtain

The stock price on any given item is mostly determined by the same old demand and supply principle that drives prices in other industries. In stock trading, this is not usually affected on a day to day basis, but over time. Scalpers, rather than look for big moves with large spreads that rarely occur look for small moves with small spreads that happen more often, increasing their chances of profiting from a sale.

c) Large Volume means Low Profits

Most scalpers will agree that this practice is not suitable for the large capital traders who are looking to move large volumes of shares at one go. This is because the profit margin that is gained from trading in shares with low spread values is negligible to the large investor. For this reason, scalping is more suited to investors who are trying to move smaller volumes more often to gain the biggest profit margins.

d) Spreads are bonuses as well as costs

As most securities exchanges worldwide operate on a bid and ask based system, and then it must be noted that the spreads between these two (the bid and the ask) do become important when you are scalping. When a trade is executed at market prices, it is important to know which side of the fence you are on. If you are the buyer, you will end up incurring costs in terms of the spread, whereas if you are the seller, you make a profit on your sale because of the spread. Sometimes holding on you your shares for a few minutes can increase their value enough that you make significant profits, but not many scalpers are willing to queue (hold on to their shares) preferring to take the small profit margin and repeat the cycle, rather than risk that margin on a 3 minute window that may yield no fruit.

These are just a few of the basic techniques used by day traders and as you can tell all of them come with their own risks and benefits. Traditional long-term investors would avoid some of these strategies as the risks seem too big to take on while the benefits would be minimal. Good day traders, on the other hand, understand that it is for precisely this reason that massive profits can be made, and, therefore, the rewards greatly outweigh the risks.

CHAPTER 5:

Day Trading Strategies

N ow that you have a sound idea of what the best day trading techniques are, you can begin to strategise so that you can make a substantial reward from all of your efforts. The ultimate goal for any day trader is to make a sizeable profit, and in order to fulfil this goal, it is necessary to control a big amount of capital.

Day traders understand that when working towards making this profit, speed and timing is everything. This is because they are focused on finding and making use of the most minute movements in stocks which have a high liquidity or index. Without the right strategy, they are unlikely to success.

A retail day trader can try out the following strategies: -

Strategy for Entry

It is not every stock on the market that is suitable for a day trader. There is a criterion that makes some stock more viable than others. A day trader will evaluate stock based on two variables. The first is the liquidity of the stock. This primarily looks at the pricing of the stock, and the ease with which a trader can enter or exit this stock. The best stock for day trading will have a tight spread, as well as a low spillage.

The second variable that a day trader will evaluate is the volatility of a stock. The mention of volatility explains movement, and in day trading, it refers to the movement in price. When evaluating volatility, the day trader takes into consideration the price range that is expected for the day. This could have two significant results, it could lead to heightened profits or significant losses.

Once liquidity and volatility have been assessed, and the stock has been identified as being appropriate for trading, the next step is to look into the best way to identify entry points.

For this, there are two tools that come in handy.

Candlestick Charts

These charts are highly popular and are essential for any day trader. They display the prices for a specific securities on a daily basis. By analysing a candlestick chart, it is possible to know the day's highest and lowest prices, as well as the opening and closing price.

In addition to this, the shape of the candle in the candlestick chart reveals more information. The section which is wide is referred to as the 'real body'. It is within this section that one can analyse the closing price in relation to the opening price, by assessing whether it was higher or lower. This is denoted by specific colours. When the stock closed at a price that was lower, the candle will be black or red in colour. However, when it closes at a price that was higher, the candle will be white or green in colour.

The shadow of the candle in this chart also tells a story. It explains the highs and lows for the day, and this can then be compared to the opening and closing prices. So in the final analysis, just the shape of the candle will vary based on all the movements taking place in a day's trade. This type of chart provides a straightforward analysis of pricing for the day.

Level II Quotes/ECN

When a gambler goes to the races, they receive a thrill by watching everything unfolding live, right before their eyes. There is an equivalent for this in day trading, and this is referred to as Level II. A trader who is using this strategy is watching the trades being executed live, right before their eyes. This is based on quotes from specific market makers. As everything unfolds, rapid decisions can be made to ensure that any small gain is capitalised on – in real time.

ECN stands for Electronic Communication Network. This is an automated system which allows traders from different locations to trade with each other easily. It works by matching buy and sell orders. This system is great for a day trader who operates as an individual because by using an ECN, the trader can actually connect directly with a major brokerage. This cuts down on fees for a middleman, and also saves time, allowing for faster and more profitable trades. The added advantage of an ECN is that trading extends beyond the typical market hours, and includes after hours trading.

In addition to these two tools, there is a chart that can prove handy when reading information for data trading. Simple being able to understand the information that is available can go a long way in creating a foundation for success.

Discerning the information from day trading transactions would be a challenge if there was no mechanism in place to make it possible. All the information from day trading is arranged in different types of trading charts. By using these trading charts, a day trader is able to keep an eye on the markets that they are trading on, and this makes it easier to make informed decisions about when they should be making their trades. It also allows them to monitor the movements on the market on a consistent basis.

There are a range of different trading charts that are available. These trading charts will all provide you with similar information, and that includes the prices that are currently being traded. Of all the available options, there are three which are referred to with heightened regularity. Candlestick charts have been discussed above. The other two are explained in this section.

Bar Charts

These are basic, easy to read charts that contain all the significant and standard trading information. This information includes but is not limited to the opening prices, closing prices and so on. The layout of the chart makes it very simple to read, and even easier to interpret. There are certain keep bits of information that are also included in the bar chart. The first of these is the open, which is an indication of the first price that was traded during the bar. Next, there is the high, which indicates the highest rice that was trading during the bar. The third piece of information is the low, which gives an idea of the lowest price that was traded during the bar. Finally, there is the close, which details the final price that was traded during the bar.

By reading these prices on the charts, one can make some conclusions about the bar. First, the inclusion of the open and close reveal whether the bar managed to close in a position that was higher than when it opened. Then, the inclusion of the high and low reveal whether the bar fell within a particular range and that range can then be analysed. This range would be the distance that can be seen between the high bar and the low bar.

Line Charts

Of the three types of charts listed here, these are the least popular. When looking at day trading charts as a whole, these are highly popular. In the same way that the other mentioned charts contain all the significant trading information, the same applies to the line charts. However, these charts have the added advantage (or disadvantage depending on your perspective) of only being supported by using charting software.

The charts that are used during trading will all have their own unique way of displaying information, and this means that they also have different ways that they should be read. This in turn will affect how they are interpreted by traders.

There is software available that makes the process of reading these charts much easier for the day trader. This software is also used for creating charts. Almost all day trading brokerages today will use charting software

Defining Stop Losses

The main aim of a trader has been established as making a profit. Day trading is exciting and thrilling. When a day trader is going through the rapid motions of the day, it is quite possible to get caught up in the speed of things and make decisions that may cost money, are reckless or have not been given due consideration.

To stay on the safe side, the trader needs to set up a stop loss order. This will help to guide the sales of the security, as a stop loss order is one where a broker is instructed to make a sale on a security one it has attained a particular price. The aim of putting this in place is to limit the loss that an investor may incur. When an investor is unable to place a significant focus on their daily trading, a stop order comes in handy, as it helps to keep the day's trading within a certain control.

A day trader who trades on margin will be the one most likely to define a stop loss. Once a day trader has determined the amount that they are willing to lose, a physical stop loss order can be put into place. If for any reason a traders entry criteria appears to be violated, then a mental stop loss set at a specific point will be triggered.

All traders need to be careful to ensure that they do not lose everything that they have in their portfolio in a day, simple because they were operating without a clear head or plan. It is imperative that a day traders should set a maximum loss for each day, especially one that will not break the bank. It should also be the type of loss that will not cripple you mentally and financially. No matter what may be happening during the day, when you reach your maximum loss, stop trading. It may be tempting to try and make up any loss in the last trades of the day, but efforts like these in the last minute will usually backfire.

Practice, Perfect, Patch-up

If you are under the impression that the moment you start day trading, having mastered the techniques mentioned earlier, you will make a significant profit, they you are highly mistaken. Have you ever seen a child learning how to get a bike? They get on it, are given a little push and before long, they fall off. They will fall off several times before they finally get it right. The only way that they can develop the skill for riding the bike is through practice.

When you go into day trading, it will be some time before you can make your profit. You will spend some time losing before things begin to pick up. You need to keep practicing the techniques in order to get things right.

Following practice, you can begin to perfect. At this point, you are improving the methodology that you have employed for beating the odds. Patching things up requires an evaluation of a person's personality, to assess whether everyone is on the same page. In day trading, the focus should be on creating a strategy for a good trade, rather than looking at profit as the end all of business.

CHAPTER 6:

Day Trading Order Types

Whenever anyone is day trading, they need to use orders to complete the trade. Each and every trade will have its own orders, and, therefore, it is vital to understand the different types of orders that exist. Through the use of these orders, a trade can be completed.

Their typical trade will have a minimum of two orders. These would be one buy order and one sell order. One of these orders will be in place for the purpose of meeting the trade, whereas the other will be based on leaving the trade.

They are characterised as single orders, and they work in tandem with each other. Therefore, if you are going into a trade with a buy order, you will have to leave the trade with a sell order.

Following these orders, there are a large number of alternatives that day traders can take advantage of when executing their trades. There are outlined as follows.

Market Orders (MKT)

When it is necessary to buy or sell a contract at the best price that is currently available, this is referred to as a market order. The market is usually quite active, and the result is the price on a market order will change quite a bit. Even though these types of orders are consistently likely to be filled, they are not likely to always be filled at the exact price that the trader was hoping for.

Limit Orders (LMT)

When it is necessary to buy or sell a contract at a price that is specific or has been defined as being a better price, this is referred to as a limit order. When the market is barely moving, then it is unlikely that a limit order will be filled. However, unlike the market order, a limit order will usually be filled at the chosen price. If a better price is available, then it will be filled at the better price.

Stop Orders (STP)

When it is necessary to buy or sell a contract at the best price that is currently available, though they can only be processed once the market has attained a particular price, then this is known as a stop order.

Any day trader will let you know that having a stop order is required. This is because of the risk that is associated with trading and doing business. This in a way helps to offer some protection from the possibility of incurring a big loss. If the order is chosen wisely, and there is sufficient knowledge of the market, then a trader cannot lose.

Stop Limit Orders (STPLMT)

This is a special type of order that combines a limit order and a stop order. This also has special conditions that need to be fulfilled in order for it to be processed. The processing will occur on condition that the market has been able to attain a particular price. This order will then change, and the processing will be done as if it were a limit order. This means that the only time it is possible for this order to he filled is when the chosen price has been attained, or a better price has become available.

Market if Touched Orders (MIT)

This type of order is unique, although it is almost identical to a stop order. What makes it different is that it is only made useful once the market price has been traded beyond the stop price. Also, the trader should be in a position where they only want to order to be processed the moment that the market price reaches the stop price.

Limit if Touched Orders (LIT)

This is another type of order that is also very similar to a stop order. It is different in that it is only utilised once the market price has been able to trade beyond the stop price. The other condition that needs to be fulfilled is that the trader is looking to have the order processed should the market price return to the stop price. It is only in this scenario that the trade can continue and be finalised.

CHAPTER 7:

The Cost of Day Trading

D ay trading can be relatively inexpensive if you use the right strategies when starting out. The right setup can really bring the cost of trading down, especially initial costs. Getting the right equipment is always going to save you some expenses from the onset of your endeavor.

There are also other things to consider such as commission, the type of brokerage firm you are using and the services you shall be engaging in to supply you with real-time market data. Using the standard free market data may seem like a good idea, but keep in mind that this information provided free tends to be delayed and this will not benefit you in any way if you are a day trader. The fact that this data can be delayed by up to 60 minutes means that for a day trader it is extremely unreliable, as even a 5 minute delay can spell disaster for your stock value if it crashes.

This chapter seeks to outline the different strategies that can be used to bring down the costs of day trading by suggesting different cost effective methods that can be used anywhere at any time. These methods have proven to be both cost-effective and productive and have helped day traders in the past realize their full potential.

1. Equipment

Now that you have decided to go into day trading the first and most important piece of equipment you are going to need is a computer and a powerful one. Day trading involves making trades rapidly, and this cannot be done on an effectively slow system.

Market makers right now are using computers that have at least 4 processing cores (like the Intel Core i5 or Core i7) with at least 8 GB RAM. These machines are top of the range and may seem a bit extravagant but as you will soon find out with day trading speed is everything.

They also come with large storage capacities, usually around 500 GB and above. This is needed because the software that you will use and the data that needs to be processed will take up a lot of space in the long term. If you get confused about what kind of machine would be best for you, a good starting point would be to go to an electronics shop that sells a range of different computers and ask for one that is suitable for gaming.

It is recommended that a backup of your system be stored on an entirely different machine, preferably a laptop. This is because when it comes to computers, just like your trading anything can happen. Should any glitches or crashes occur, you want to be able to switch seamlessly to another device to continue trading or at least have your broker's app on your phone to allow you to stay up to date with the market. Another advantage of having your backup on a laptop is so that if you are travelling anywhere, you can stay in touch with the markets via your laptop, as most phone apps will not allow you to have as much control as a full program will.

An array of monitors is also recommended. Two screens are good enough, and four is even better, but the best results have come from systems with six to eight monitors. These give you the ability to see all the information clearly and make quicker, better-informed decisions on the stocks you are trading. The computer and monitor array may seem expensive with the top of the range setups costing about US$ 3,000 and the cheaper options costing US$ 1,700, but for serious day traders, these things are vital as the speed of your transactions is intricately related to the speed of your machine.

The software will also play a significant role, as every serious trader these days uses software to buy and sell securities. When choosing what software to use, it is always important to make sure that the software you are using is widely used, well-known, and relevant when it comes to whatever asset class you are interested in trading in.

The software should also have the following components:

- *Level II* – This is a list of all the buyers and sellers on the market

- *Time And Sales Data* – This is a time-stamped record of all transactions carried out

- *Real Time Streaming Of Quotes And Charts:* A live feed of all market data

- *A Portfolio Tracker:* This will help keep track of your stocks

The software can be very expensive, with some programs being sold at upwards of US$ 5,000. Others charge you per trade or transaction that you carry out. It is important to carry out your own in-depth research to help you choose the right program to fit your needs.

A high-speed internet connection is also important and goes without saying. The most common connection is the Cable Modem Internet Connection though the ideal service to get for trading would be the Fibre Optic Internet Service. Cable internet will supply you with internet speeds of up to 100 Mbps, which is more than fast enough to do basic trading online, but fibre optic internet can provide you with speeds that are ten times as fast. For traders like scalpers who need to have low latency internet, fibre optics is the way to go.

Fibre optic internet is still a relatively new phenomenon, so it is not yet available everywhere, but if it is available in your area it is highly recommended if you want to become a day trader.

2. Brokerage and Commission

Brokerage is an important factor when it comes to day traders as different types of brokers have different ways of doing things and different commission charges.

For instance, market maker brokers though still faster than the traditional brokerage firms are slow to execute trades. For a day trader, the faster the transaction can happen and the lower the commission, the better. Market makers can be slow, especially if they feel more inclined to trade against the order flow for whatever reason. They also charge relatively high commissions for their services bringing down whatever profits you had envisioned making.

On the other hand, discount traders do not share this problem as they charge slight commissions to their clients. The only downside apart from the fact that they are also slow is that they offer very few services and very little support for the client, so a more comprehensive knowledge of the securities exchange market is required if you want to trade through them.

The best option for a day trader when it comes to the brokerage is the direct-access brokers who allow you to trade directly with the ECNs. The result of this is instantaneous feedback from the ECNs and transaction spends that can be measured in fractions of a second. Direct-access brokers are especially useful to scalpers who rely on speed to make the most of their investments.

The average commission rates are about US$ 5 per transaction though on the upper end of the scale commissions of US$ 10 are not uncommon. Unlike retail traders though, direct-access traders charge less commission per unit volume sold. So for instance if the commission on a transaction was US$ 5 for the round trip, a direct-access broker may charge as little as US$ 0.01 per share traded (if more than a stipulated number of shares is traded)

CHAPTER 8:

Day Trading and Technology

With more and more people venturing into day trading on their own, the use of day trading software has soared in popularity. In fact, many associate day trading with someone who sits in front of their computer all day with numbers moving around and changing.

The use of software can help any day trader increase their profits while also reaching out to traders around the globe. In addition to more individual day traders depending on software, brokerage firms are also taking advantage of software and offering their services over the internet.

The day trading software allows a day trader to carry out all trading activities on their own quickly and efficiently. When a day trader attempts to go through all the necessary processed on their own, they may discover that it is difficult to achieve any type of profit. With an automated software, this becomes considerably easier.

There is one aspect of trading using software that should be taken into consideration. That is making sure that you are using the right software.

Day Trading Software Attributes

Any software that you choose for day trading should have the following attributes.

- The moment that you want to begin trading, the software that you are using should require you to follow a one-step setup process. Through this process, you will put in place some parameters that explain your preferred trading strategy. These parameters include the trading limits that you intent to guide you, ensuring that the system can connect to live data, and allowing it to execute trades on your behalf.

- As you progress in your day trading, you can begin to add even more features to your online trading experience. These include provision for the software to use a stop loss feature.

- Your software should be on an independent platform, preferably one that is web based. This allows you to connect to a site from anywhere, and it also cuts a lot of costs. These costs include maintenance of the software, as well as costs associated with upgrades.

- You should be able to try out a trial version of the software before you make a commitment to use or purchase it. Consider the information that you want to be made available to you as a day trader. You can then set the software to track stocks and give you information on binary options for example.

Setting yourself up

There are certain tools that you need to have to successfully day trade as an individual trader. These are minimum requirements. As you go along and increase in your skills, you will be able to make use of some tools which are more specialised. To begin with, you should have the following: -

- A Computer using the most current operating system available. For now, that would be Windows 8.1. If you are just starting out, a standard computer will work perfectly for you. If you are more advanced and are running your own software, you many need something more specialised. This type of computer would require a very large hard drive. To keep track of everything happening on day trading platforms, you may need to have at least eight screens (monitors) to view.

  - o Minimum requirements for your standard PC include a good processor, 2GB Ram, at least 100 GB hard drive, 15" screen size and a network interface (10/100 Mbps).

- High-Speed Internet Access (Day trading is very time bound, so if you have a slow connection, you may be setting yourself up for failure).

- A telephone (You will occasionally need to speak directly with your broker for advice or to give direction).

- Direct Access Brokerage – Allowing you to get your hands on stocks directly without having to go through a middle man,

- Real Time Market Date – Providing you with live information on what is transpiring in day trading markets.

- Day Trading Software – This is software that will provide you information on charting to make it easier for you to track movements.

- Charting Software – You will need this type of software to help you to keep an eye on the markets. This is perhaps the most important software that you can have because it is the one that you shall be using the most. It is able to provide you information on what has happened in the page, and what is happening currently. The results are usually displayed graphically for ease of use.

- A Good Broker – Even though this may not be described as something technology-based, having a good broker is vital towards becoming a successful trader. When you start off as a day trader, you have limited knowledge. On almost all sites, it is necessary to have the details of a broker to ensure that trades can be completed. What is imperative is to search for a broker who will not swamp you with commission fees.

CHAPTER 9:

Day Trading Mistakes to Avoid

Whenever you are starting any venture, you are likely to lose something or make some mistakes before you get a proper grasp of what you are doing. This is especially true for day trading though with day trading the risks are higher. Here, the risks have to do with money, and this in itself is a challenge. This is because a day trader needs to be quick witted as well as skilful, to be able to purchase stocks and sell them within the same day, and hope that by doing so it is possible to make a profit from the minutest fluctuations in the prices of the stock over 12 hours.

Years ago, day trading was impossible for the average investor, as the tools that were needed were not available to them. These tools included real-time stock results, access to instant traders and the tools for analysis. High-speed internet and Dutch courage have changed this scenario for many who are now willing to try their hand at day trading. There are some things that need to be avoided though, even for the most strong-hearted new trader.

In day trading, making mistakes should be avoided as much as possible because even the slightest mistake can have a massive impact on total income. In order to avoid mistakes, you need to be aware of the mistakes that you could inadvertently make. That is what will be addressed in this section.

Starting Big

As a new day trader, it is likely that you are bubbling with enthusiasm as you look forward to starting your trades. You have read up on all the theory, including the trips and tricks and believe that you are ready for the game. If you have managed a sizeable capital portfolio from an investment, you may be keen to start big, make big profits and please your client.

Even with all the theoretical preparation possible, as a new trader, you need to learn and observe the practical aspects of day trading. With experience, you can take calculated risks.

For this reason, new day traders are advised to start small rather than starting big. This is because when you are likely to make the most significant mistakes in your trading career as you start out. If you have invested in something which has lost you a large amount of money for the client, they you will likely affect your career for the considerable future.

You need to start trading with capital that is minimal so that you can assess your success. After a while, and with your wits intact, you should be able to see successful trading with more than 3 contracts. At this point, you can consider increasing the amount of money that you invest each time, and this should help you get better profits.

Learn the Basics

Day trading is not something that you can simply teach yourself and then start excelling at. You need to get some hands-on advice from people who are seasoned day traders. To do this, you should find an experienced trader and spend some time observing them, asking questions and listening to advice. Learn how to play the game of trading, so that you can build up the confidence to give it a good go yourself. Realise that this will require patience on your part, so that it can be gotten right. With proper determination, you will find that your efforts are enough to lead to big profits.

Planning To Fail

Failing to plan is planning to fail, and this is especially true for day traders. Trading is about making a profit, and not about experiencing feelings of exhilaration by taking chances with money. In light of the outcome that is expected, it is important that all traders have a plan of action.

A plan is particularly important because of the speed and emotion that affects day trading. Day trading are likely to be backed into corners where they need to make instant decisions, or during a volatile day of trading, they could get caught up in the events of the day and make decisions that will negatively affect their bottom line. Have a plan in place, especially when it is in writing, is an important step to controlling day trading.

A day trader, who has taken the time to create a plan which is detailed, will understand what his overall goal will be and will mould behaviour and actions to meet that goal. Within the plan, there should be information on what shall be traded and the markets that the trades will take place in. There will also be details on the methods that will be used for entry and exit into the markets. This will help the day trader avoid buying into a security which would not usually have been considered.

An excellent plan will also have a risk assessment section, with details on the proper reactions to a host of scenarios. This could include how to react adequately to an excellent day of trading, or how to deal with consistent disappointments. Either way, it is supposed to ensure that the trader remains on track regarding what is required.

Missing Discipline

The best managers, especially those who work in high-risk professions will often create a contingency plan, in case their original plan does not pan out. This means that they are ready for the unexpected.

In day trading, this type of planning is also necessary, particularly because, this activity is highly emotional. Having discipline could be the difference between profit and loss.

An aspect of discipline includes stop-loss orders. These orders are triggered based on certain conditions within the day trading market. They help investors to save money, particularly if the trade is taking place automatically. It is imperative that all traders have a plan that will help them to manage their risks, as well as their possibilities for success or failure.

Manage your Expectations

Day trading is not a get rich quick scheme. Neither is it a magical wand that will help relieve all of your problems. It is challenging, and there is the constant pressure that you could lose it all.

Rather than expecting to rake in the dollars, expect to put in significant amount of work in to perfect the method in which you trade. The reason for this is that success in trading requires a considerable amount of planning, together with hard work.

This planning requires an adequate input of time. Ideally, the time should be well spend observing leaders in the industry so as to discern their techniques.

Being Time Bad

Day trading is already chaotic because of the speed with which transactions are done. However, there is no time that is as busy and chaotic as the first and last 20 minutes of each day. This is because it is the period where investors are the most anxious, looking to make the fastest moves before everyone else appears, or at the end of the day.

As a new trader, this is an excellent example of volatility in the market. It would serve you better to simply wait, rather than join the hubbub. This way, you prevent yourself from making any detrimental mistakes, and you keep away from the competition from institutional traders.

Keeping Too Busy

Being busy is important, and many people want to be observed as being busy, as this is a way that they can validate the amount of work that they have had to do. In trading, being too busy is not good for a trader, it indicates that it is possible to let things slip through their fingers.

A new trader may attempt to manage at least 10 trades in a day. The assumption is by trading more, you can make more. This may not actually be the case. Some professional traders insist on trading just two traders through the day. They may complete the trades early in the day, but then they can spend the rest of the day following up. By having fewer day trades to monitor, it becomes easier to see when there is a change in the market.

If you are a new trader and have achieved success from doing two trades a day, you may be tempted to make more money by increasing the number of investors and trading more. The problem with this is that it may set you back and turn your profitability on its head. This is because you will be stretching your attention. Instead, try increasing the amount that you are trading on your two commodities or for your two investors.

Watch out for Losing Streaks

There is nothing that can be as disheartening as repeatedly losing when you are day trading. If you are not careful, it may reach the point where you end up being clinically depressed, especially if you are always losing more progressively. That is why even though you may have the enthusiasm to day trade on your own, you need to seek out council from a professional who has been successful. Over time, you will pass the phase of losing streaks, and the moments that you were demoralised will be distant memories.

Thinking Anyone Can Do It

Should you ever be in a car accident, and were in need of life-saving surgery, would you allow a teenager in high school to operate on you? Your answer is most likely "Absolutely Not!!"

If you had a large sum of money which you wanted to see grow, would you pass it to the first person that you walk by on the street and say, "I'll wait to hear from you," – highly unlikely.

So when you are looking for a day trader, you need to make sure on certain things, one of which is that the person is qualified when it comes to day trading. They need to have some training as well as possible certification. If you have made the decision to go into day trading without any help, then you also need to ensure that you are capable of making informed decisions. Make sure that you have mastered all the theoretical properties possible and that you have watched an expert practically as well. Remember that you cannot rush the process. It is entirely possible that this could take several months.

Keep an Eye on your Risk Capital

There is every possibility that when you are trading your capital, that you will lose everything. This means that you need to be able to distinguish between your normal capital and your trading capital. Your normal capital includes the money that you need for your day to day living, so that you can pay bills have food to eat, pay your rent or mortgage and have something decent stashed away for your retirement. Your trading capital is money that you are willing to risk. This is money that should be solely dedicated to day trading, and nothing else. That way, it you lose it all, your life will not start to fall apart all around you. It is also noteworthy that a day trader is required to keep a certain amount in their account as equity, and the minimum must be maintained if there is to be any day trading taking place.

Messing up your Margin

Your capital as a day trader is likely to fluctuate up and down through-out the day. Sometimes it is on the lower side, and you need an extra boost. So you choose to borrow from a broker so that you can pur-chase securities. This is meant to be a facility that gives day traders some wiggle room if it is used correctly. However, some people have used this support in the wrong way or have abused it. This could occur when one borrows much more than they can pay back, and the result is an empty trading account and the mounting of debt. As much as possible, day traders should trade within their means.

Ignoring Important Resources

Perhaps the most important asset that you can get that will lead you to success when day trading online is an excellent high-speed internet connection. Next, is an investment in state of the art software that is specialised and fully loaded with a range of analysis tools. Then you should make sure that your trading wallet is well stocked, as you need a significant amount of capital to get you started. As part of your re-sources, you should have direct access to an expert in the field so that you can get advice when you need it, and also get input on your equip-ment and its specifications. Finally, hire yourself a coach. This will be a great investment, allowing you to learn what is necessary to master day trading for the long haul.

Forgetting About Mental Health

Having the right state of mind could be the difference between winning and losing. In order to come out on top as a winner, one who is competent and can trade on instinct, you need to learn how you can manage your emotions. So you cannot allow the intense thinking and mental energy that goes into day trading bring you down and drain your energy. You have to be ready for action, always ready to make a move now. This is like having a jerk reflex. With this as a trick up your sleeve, you will be able to gain competence and win consistently. It will build up your intuition so that you always aim for and attain trading success.

The more that you trade, the better you will become. You need to give yourself the gift of concentration when you being trading. This is so that you can create sweet trading music in your mind. Getting into the zone is something that the most successful traders are able to. It is the trance of trading, and it leads to success.

www.ingramcontent.com/pod-product-compliance
Lightning Source LLC
Chambersburg PA
CBHW070300190526
45169CB00001B/482